THIS JOURNAL BELONGS TO

ONE BADASS SUPERHUMAN

ACKNOWLEDGEMENT

THIS SUPERJOURNAL WOULDN'T EXIST WITHOUT SOME TRULY EXTRAORDINARY ASS-KICKING PEOPLE STEPPING IN.

AROUND EVERY PAGE TURN IS THE DEDICATION, HARD WORK, AND POSITIVE PROFANITY FROM ONE OUTSTANDING SUPERHERO WHO TRANSFORMED THIS BOOK INTO SOMETHING VERY SPECIAL TO ME. SHE IS THE GREATEST SIDEKICK I COULD EVER ASK FOR IN LIFE.

INTRODUCTION

Welcome, superhuman! You're about to start the adventure of a lifetime where you'll learn a shit-ton about what makes you so awesome, discover your hidden superpowers, and plan your epic journey towards making the world a better place, one bad-guy-ass-kicking at a time.

Do you feel like your current day-to-day grind is sucking the soul from your body, slowly turning you into a mindless zombie waiting for its next meal? Maybe you're a fully functioning human being who *actually* has some of their shit together (**FIST BUMP!**). Either way, I'm going to show you that you're more badass than you think you are.

You've got skills. **YOU CAN DO STUFF!** You've got a strong heart and a sound mind. Well, maybe your mind's a little frazzled, jaded, dazed and confused… **THAT'S OK!** Often, those who feel the most fucked up end up being the world-changers that we so desperately need. So, no matter how you're feeling right now, I'm here for you! Together, we're gonna kick some ass, get shit done and launch you into the sparkly **plains of otherworldliness.**

PLAINS OF OTHERWORLDLINESS

A magical and mystical place, often mentioned in folklore, where you're finally doing the thing that you're meant to do with your life. Produces tingly sensations of glorious euphoria, not unlike that of blissfully sauntering through a glistening, dewy meadow as your fingertips deftly brush the tips of the pussy willows, all the while leaping and bounding your way towards that celestial pot of gold at the end of a rainbow.

Fuck the F Word
Get Declusterfucked
Exhale Bullshit
Fuckit
Balls to the Wall
Reach Your Rewardgasm
FUCK
FEAR
B

HEY, I'M BRAVEBUD!

SUPERPOWERS

Firewords: I'll light you up inside like a New Year's fireworks display with my profane-yet-positive vocabulary.

Fog Vision: I can see through the thickest layers of your brain-fog and help you visualize your future crystal clear.

SPECIAL WEAPONS

Fear-Fucking Blasters: Blast the fuck out of your limiting beliefs, self-doubts, and any other fears that stand in your way.

Truthbombs: For when you need to hear the cold, hard truth.

B – BOLD ACTION WILL CHANGE YOUR LIFE
Progress starts with taking small steps RIGHT NOW!

R – REWIRE YOUR WAY OF THINKING
You become what you think about.

A – ADVENTURE INTO THE KNOWN
Learn from those who are doing what you want to do.

V – ADD MASSIVE VALUE TO OTHERS
Use your superpowers to make a positive impact.

E – ENJOY THE PROCESS
Enjoy doing, failing, growing and finding new ways to kick ass.

BUD
All you need is just one person to believe in you and that's me!

CONTENTS

LET'S BLOW THIS POPSICLE STAND!

THE SUPERHERO WITHIN
CH 1
PURPOSE
"There is a superhero in all of us, we just need the courage to put on the cape."
- Superman

SUPERHERO INTAKE FORM

HEY THERE, KICK-ASS PERSON! LET'S GET TO KNOW A LITTLE MORE ABOUT YOUR SEXY, MAGNIFICENT SELF:

Superpowers you might have?

____

Are you willing to wear spandex?

____

If the government gave you the power to fly, run super fast, and control minds but you'd have to do a few favors for them with your new powers, would you accept?

____

If you could choose one superhero to have an epic kissing scene with who would you choose?

____

Would you rather have scissors for hands or flippers for feet?

____

If you were building a superteam, which 5 superheroes (or villains) would you put on your team?

____

Favorite superhero?

____

Sexiest superhero?

____

Most hated villain?

____

If you could choose one body part that could be super stretchy, which one would you choose?

____

Do you struggle with any of the following phobias?

1. Arachibutyrophobia –Fear of peanut butter sticking to the roof of your mouth ☐
2. Xanthophobia –Fear of the color yellow ☐
3. Ablutophobia –Fear of bathing ☐
4. Octophobia –Fear of the number eight ☐
5. Syngenesophobia –Fear of relatives ☐
6. Papaphobia –Fear of the Pope ☐
7. Kinemortophobia –Fear of zombies ☐
8. Anatidaephobia –Fear of being watched by a duck ☐
9. Lycraphobia –Fear of spandex ☐
10. Masklophobia –Fear of costumed characters or people in masks ☐

TOTAL SCORE = ◯

Resilient Honest Bodacious Exceptional
Loved DANGEROUS Funny
Beautiful Brave Confident GANGSTA
Sexy Determined High Class
I'M FUCKING...
Courageous Smart Unique
Shagtacular Badass
Strong Needed Gritty Batman
Legendary THE BOMB Inspirational
BITCH STICK
NO BS

9 TIMES OUT OF 10, THE BIGGEST ENEMY THAT BEATS US DOWN IS OUR OWN NEGATIVE SELF.

CUT THAT SHIT OUT!

HAVING A POSITIVE MINDSET ABOUT WHO YOU ARE IS EVERYTHING WHEN IT COMES TO BEING A SUPERHERO.

Write down and color in all the words that represent the downright awesome human you are.

What's Your
Krytponite?
Jugs and Thugs
Cola

Every hero has a weakness that makes them feel like a spineless bottom-feeder. What bad habits are you hooked to that are total garbage? Netflix binging, booze, social media scrolling, fast food? List at least 3 below.

How would your life be better by reducing or eliminating that crap?

What strategies can you think of to overcome them?

WHAT ARE YOU FIGHTING FOR?

MORE AND MORE THESE DAYS, PEOPLE DON'T ENJOY THEIR DAY JOBS. QUITE SIMPLY, THEY'RE NOT PASSIONATE ABOUT THE FIGHT THEY'RE IN. WOULD YOU RISK GETTING THE SHIT BEATEN OUT OF YOU BY FIGHTING SOMEONE WHO ISN'T WORTH YOUR DAMN TIME? **HELL NO** YOU WOULDN'T! SO WHY IS IT THAT PEOPLE WILLINGLY BEAT THEMSELVES UP (MENTALLY, EMOTIONALLY, MORALLY) BY STAYING AT JOBS THEY DON'T LIKE?

DOING STUFF THAT YOU'RE RED-HOT PASSIONATE ABOUT IS WORTH YOUR TIME.

DO YOU KNOW WHAT THAT EVEN FEELS LIKE? MAYBE YOU HAVEN'T A DAMN CLUE OF WHAT SETS YOU ON FIRE.

NEWS FLASH YOU'RE NOT ALONE!

WHAT'S IMPORTANT IS THAT YOU BEGIN TRYING NEW EXPERIENCES UNTIL YOU STUMBLE UPON SOMETHING THAT MAKES YOU SAY

"Holy shit, where have you been all my life?!"

ANSWER THE QUESTIONS BELOW AND MAKE SURE TO DO A **BIG EXPLOSIVE BRAIN DUMP** ALL OVER THE PLACE. MAYBE YOU'RE ONE OF THE LUCKY DUCKS THAT'S ALREADY FIGURED OUT WHAT YOU WANT TO DO WITH YOUR LIFE - CONGRATS! WRITE IT DOWN AND GET REAL SPECIFIC.

What are some things that, while doing, I completely lose track of time?

____

____

____

____

____

____

What did I love doing as a teenager? (Classes, hobbies, activities)

____

____

____

____

____

____

____

What causes are important to me?

____

____

____

____

____

____

What do I love giving advice on?

____

____

____

____

____

____

From your brain dump above, what are 1–2 possible side hustles that you could start pursuing today? Anything is possible!

____

____

OVER THE YEARS, YOU BEGIN DISCOVERING NEW TALENTS, HOBBIES, AND INTERESTS THAT NEVER APPEALED TO YOU BEFORE. THAT, MY FRIEND, IS CALLED **GROWTH**, AND YOU BEST BELIEVE THAT YOU AND EVERY OTHER HUMAN EXPERIENCES IT!

MAYBE YOU'RE ONE OF THOSE WEIRDOS WHO'S CRAZY GOOD AT BUILDING TINY KITCHENS TO COOK TINY MEALS FOR TINY HAMSTERS (LOOK IT UP, IT'S REALLY REAL). PERHAPS YOU LIKE SCALING WALLS AND SHIT WITH YOUR BARE HANDS AND JUMPING OFF OF BUILDINGS SHOUTING **"PARKOUR!"** OR, MAYBE YOU'RE JUST THE MOST BIG-HEARTED S.O.B. WHO GETS ALL WARM AND FUZZY INSIDE BEING A COMPANION TO LONELY ELDERLY FOLKS. NO MATTER WHAT YOUR GIFTS ARE OR WHAT MAKES YOUR BIG HEART SWELL, THEY'RE YOUR SUPERPOWERS THAT MAKE YOU UNIQUELY **YOU**.

No matter how insignificant they might seem, there's a purpose behind the powers you've been given.

YOU'RE A ONE-OF-A-KIND SUPERHUMAN WHO'S MEANT TO DO SOME IMPORTANT SHIT!

BS-RAY VISION

The ability to see through people's bullshit. Perfect for lawyers and bewildered parents everywhere.

WONDER FINGERS

Lightning fast fingers that can type at the speed of light. Excellent for bloggers or book writers.

KARAOKE BRAIN

The ability to bust out any song lyrics at the drop of a hat. Handy for any musician.

SERENITY NOW

The ability to instantly manifest feelings of calm and tranquility for yourself and others amidst life's shitstorms. A great superpower for yoga instructors, therapists, and kindergarten teachers.

BARGAIN BOUNTY HUNTER

The ability to track down an amazing deal from miles away. Nice for those who want to start their own pawn shop reality TV show.

KITCHEN SCISSOR HANDS

The ability to instantly change your hands into any kitchen utensil and shoot spices out of your fingertips. Fantastic for wannabe chefs!

FUNNY BONE

The ability to nudge people with your funny bone and instantly make them pee themselves with laughter. Perfect for aspiring comedians.

SUPER SLOW-MO

The ability to slow down everyone and everything around you to more fully enjoy life. Excellent for newlyweds and nearly-deads.

3D PRINTER MIND

The ability to imagine something and have it be instantly created in front of you. Great for artists, inventors and architects.

IT'S TIME TO DISCOVER YOUR SUPERPOWERS! Reflect on what you're fucking awesome at (exercise 2) and think about what you're fighting for (exercise 3) and mash those together to create your superpowers.

Think about what abilities or powers you might need for what you're fighting for. Maybe there are things you've always wanted to try – what are those? You just never know which could become your strongest superpowers.

____

____

____

____

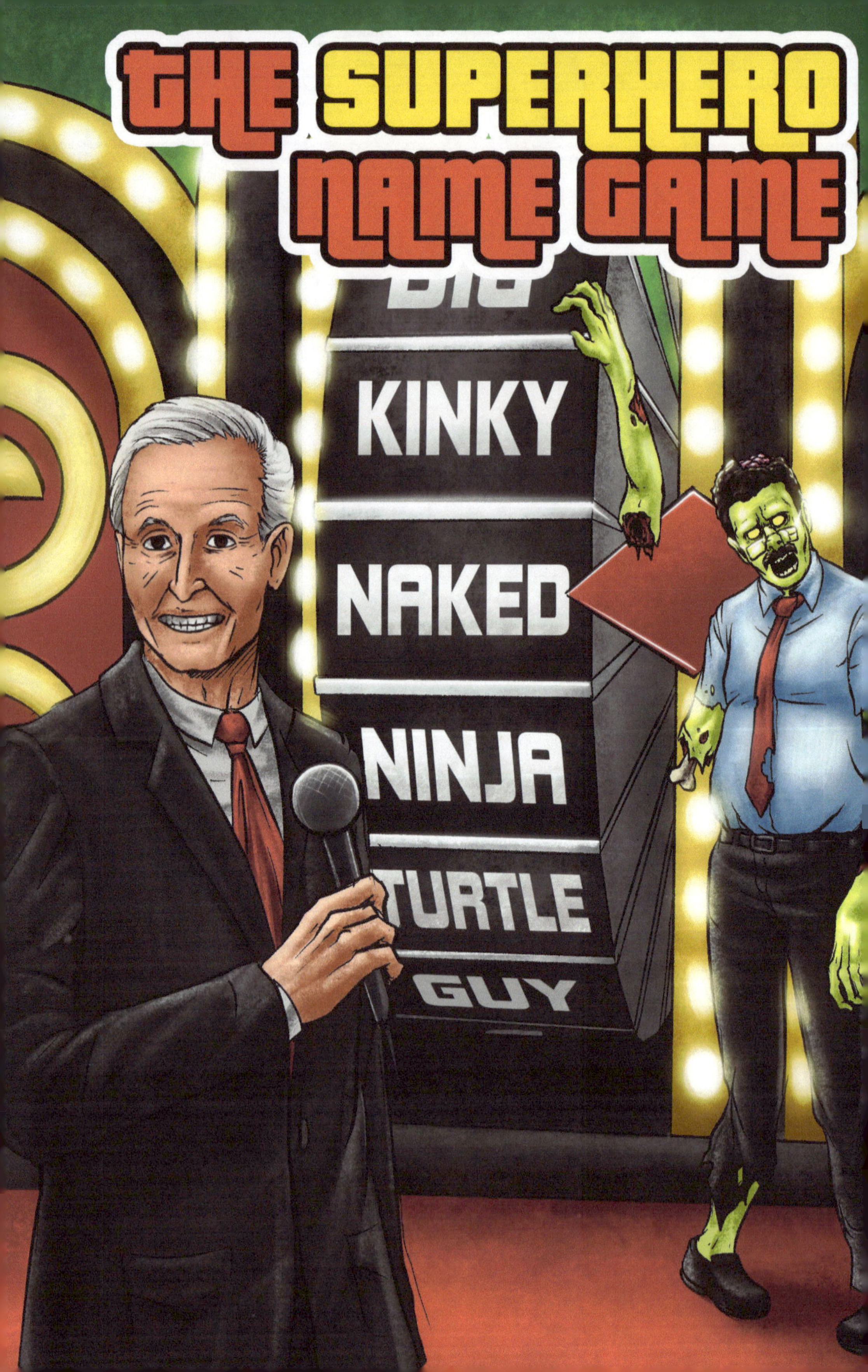

THE SUPERHERO
NAME GAME
KINKY
NAKED
NINJA
TURTLE
GUY

Pick the first letter of your first name

A = Agent	G = Gigantic	M = Mr./Mrs.	S = Super	Y = Yodeling
B = Big	H = Hot	N = Naked	T = The	Z = Zesty
C = Captain	I = Invisible	O = Officer	U = Ultra	
D = Dr.	J = Jolly	P = Pimpin'	V = Venomous	
E = Electric	K = Kinky	Q = Quiet	W = Wild	
F = Flirty	L = Lord/Lady	R = Ripped	X = XXX Rated	

First letter of your middle name

A = Aerodynamic	G = Geriatric	M = Moustached	S = Savage	Y = Yellow
B = Bitchin'	H = Hypnotic	N = Ninja	T = Tenacious	Z = Zippy
C = Caffeinated	I = Immortal	O = Oozey	U = Urban	
D = Diapered	J = Jurassic	P = Polite	V = Voluptuous	
E = Epic	K = Kick-Ass	Q = Quirky	W = Waterproof	
F = Fucking	L = Lusty	R = Raunchy	X = Xylophonic	

and the first letter of your last name

A = Angel of Death	G = Guy/Girl	M = Mutant	S = Sex Machine	Y = Yankee
B = Bear	H = Hipster	N = Nacho	T = Turtle	Z = Zebra
C = Cactus	I = Imposter	O = Octopus	U = Unicorn	
D = Devil	J = Juggernaut	P = Panda	V = Velociraptor	
E = Elf	K = Kangeroo	Q = Quail	W = Warrior	
F = Fox	L = Lover	R = Robot	X = XXX Pornstar	

Superhero Name

Okay, okay. You don't have to use this name, but make sure you come up with one that makes you feel fucking super!

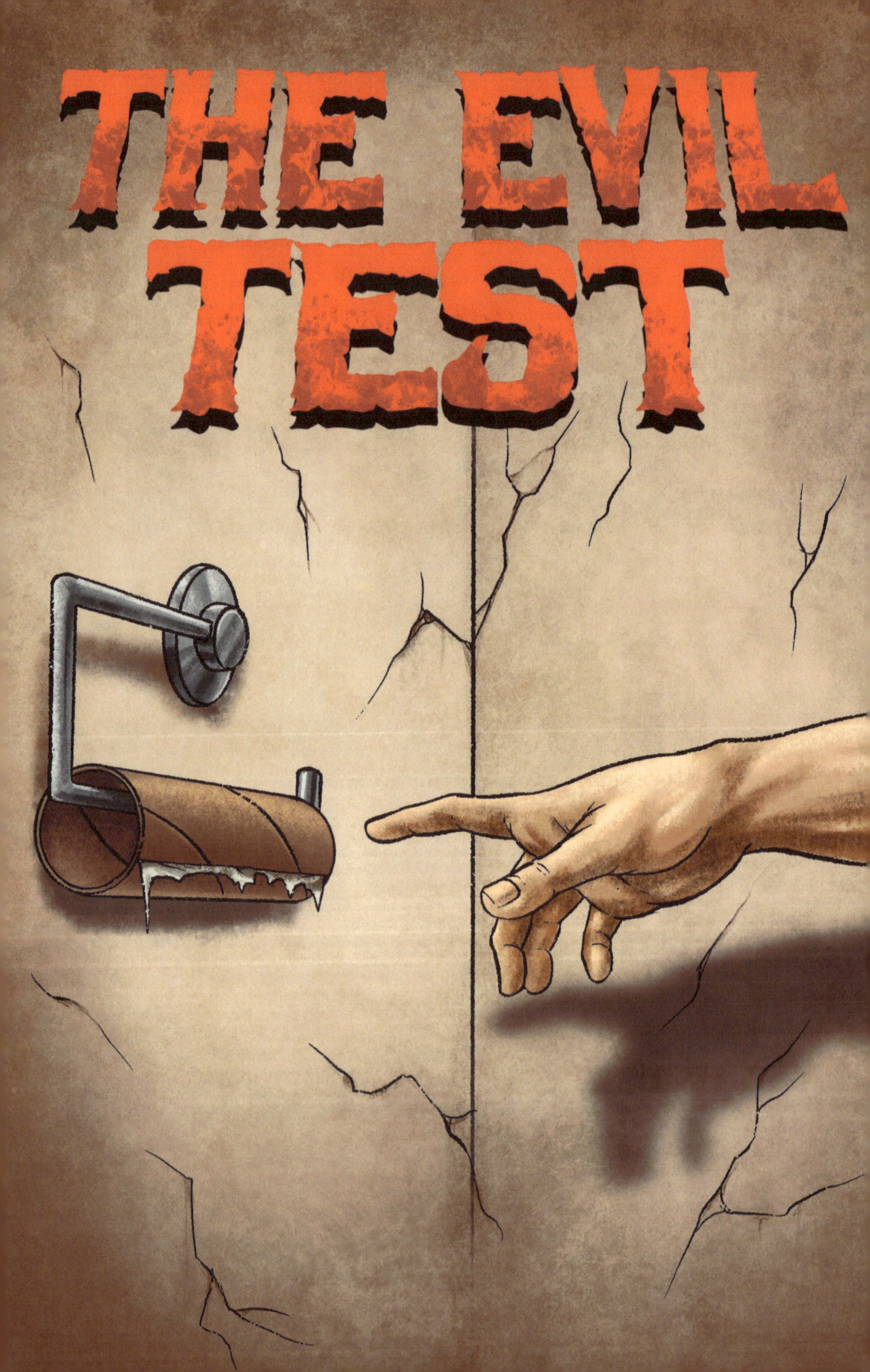

THE EVIL
TEST

IT'S TIME TO FACE THE MUSIC AND SEE HOW EVIL YOU REALLY ARE... FINGERS CROSSED!

Have you ever:

1. Farted in an elevator with others inside ☐
2. Intentionally cut someone off while driving for no good reason and felt like a winner ☐
3. Peed in a swimming pool ☐
4. Knocked something over by accident in a store and bolted before anyone saw you ☐
5. Ate all of someone else's leftovers without telling them ☐
6. Cheated on a school test ☐
7. Stole something from a store ☐
8. Turned off someone's video game system mid-game before they could save it ☐
9. Finished off the toilet paper roll and didn't replace it ☐
10. Cheered for the bad guy to win in a superhero movie ☐

Score: ⬤

9-10: DAMN... YOU EVIL! You have all the makings of a super villain. Please come back to the good side, we need you!

7-8: EVIL COULD BE YOUR MIDDLE NAME. You're treading on thin ice. Don't risk plunging yourself into darkness!

4-6: WEE-VIL. A little bit devilish, mostly angelic. Good enough!

0-3: YOU'RE A SAINT. So shiny, so pure! Keep on being the blindingly bright beacon of light that you are!

I STAND FOR

JUSTICE? LOVE? PEACE? GLORYHOLES?

WHEN WAS THE LAST TIME YOU THOUGHT ABOUT YOUR VALUES? VALUES ARE THE GUARDRAILS THAT HELP YOU MAKE BIG AND SMALL DECISIONS IN LIFE, AND HOPEFULLY PREVENT YOU FROM PEEING IN SWIMMING POOLS, FARTING IN ELEVATORS, AND STEALING PUPPIES.

1. Check off below any of the values that resonate with you and fill in the blanks with any other words that you live by:

Acceptance ☐	Fun ☐	Positivity ☐	______
Accountability ☐	Generosity ☐	Proactivity ☐	______
Adventure ☐	Growth ☐	Reliability ☐	______
Boldness ☐	Happiness ☐	Resilience ☐	______
Community ☐	Honesty ☐	Risk-taking ☐	______
Compassion ☐	Humility ☐	Selflessness ☐	______
Contribution ☐	Humor ☐	Simplicity ☐	______
Creativity ☐	Individuality ☐	Spirituality ☐	______
Excellence ☐	Kindness ☐	Wealth ☐	______
Family ☐	Leadership ☐	Well-being ☐	______

2. Select 4 words from the above list that are most important to you:

3. Add a verb/action to the beginning of each of your words and who it affects:

I stand for multiplying happiness in the lives of others	I stand for always paying attention to my well-being	I stand for continually focusing on my growth	I stand for resilience in the face of any challenges
I stand for	I stand for	I stand for	I stand for

WHETHER YOU LIKE IT OR NOT, MOST OF YOUR BELIEFS AS AN ADULT FORMED BECAUSE OF THE BLUEPRINTS YOUR PARENTS/PRIMARY CAREGIVERS CREATED IN YOUR MIND AS A CHILD. KNOWING WHO YOU ARE AND WHY YOU ACT THE WAY YOU DO REQUIRES YOU TO PULL OUT THESE BLUEPRINTS, DUST THEM OFF, AND REALIZE **YOU ARE IN CONTROL** OF CHANGING THEM AT ANY TIME.

Answer the following questions with what *immediately* comes to mind:

Which one of your parents love/approval did you crave more as a child? ___________

What did you have to be or do to gain their approval and love?

I had to be/do ____

____

____

____

____

____

THE REALITY IS THESE BELIEFS ALSO FORMED STRESSORS AND ANXIETY IN YOU, LIKE WORRYING ABOUT NOT LIVING UP TO THESE PERCEIVED STANDARDS. THEY'RE ALSO A BIG REASON FOR SOME OF THE NEGATIVE HABITS AND BEHAVIORS YOU MAY HAVE FORMED THROUGHOUT YOUR LIFE. EVER WONDER WHY IN MOVIES YOU ALWAYS SEE THE PSYCHIATRIST ASKING THEIR PATIENT ABOUT WHAT THEIR CHILDHOOD WAS LIKE? SO MUCH OF WHO YOU ARE TODAY AND WHAT YOU BELIEVE IN STEMS FROM YOUR UPBRINGING.

THESE BELIEFS ARE THE BIGGEST REASON **WHY** YOU DO WHAT YOU DO; THEY HAVE SHAPED YOUR IDENTITY. RECOGNIZE WHEN THESE ARE NEGATIVELY AND POSITIVELY INFLUENCING YOUR THOUGHT PATTERNS AND YOU'LL INSTANTLY BE ABLE TO ADJUST YOUR MINDSET IN A MORE POSITIVE DIRECTION. (MORE TO COME IN CH. 2)

"Identity is a prison you can never escape, but the way to redeem your past is not to run from it, but to try to understand it, and use it as a foundation to grow." - *Jay Z*

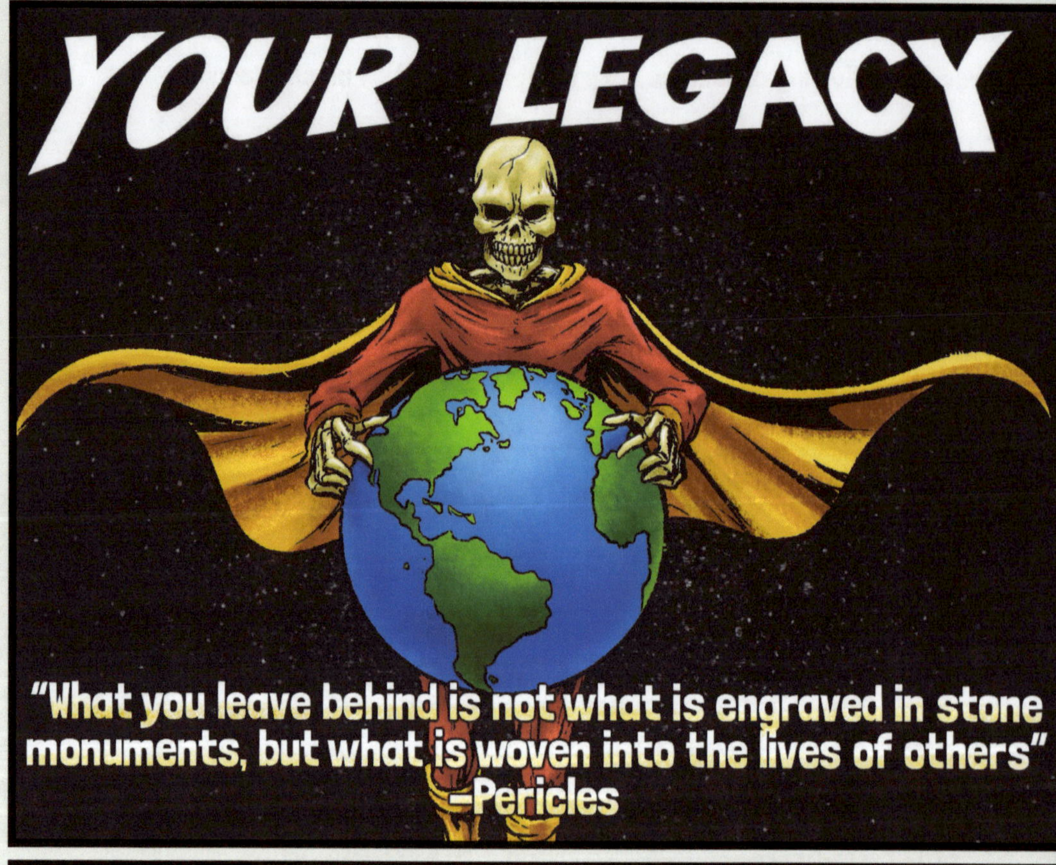

YOUR LEGACY: WHEN'S THE LAST TIME YOU THOUGHT ABOUT IT? HAVE YOU EVER? WHAT EVEN IS A LEGACY? IT'S THE MARK YOU LEAVE ON THIS PLANET BEFORE YOUR HOURGLASS EMPTIES. YOU CAN EITHER GIVE THE WORLD A BEAUTIFUL TATTOO OR AN UGLY SCAR.

SORRY TO BE THE BEARER OF BAD NEWS, BUT DEATH IS COMING FOR YOU ONE DAY. THINK ABOUT THE POSITIVE IMPACT YOU WANT TO LEAVE ON THE WORLD, AND HOW YOU'D LIKE TO MAKE PEOPLE FEEL WHENEVER THEY THINK ABOUT YOU.

How do you want to be remembered when you're dead and gone?

____

____

____

____

____

____

What would you like your great-great-great-grandchildren to read about you one day?

____

____

____

____

____

____

____

____

HOW YOU'LL SAVE THE WORLD

THE MOST VITAL PART OF UNDERSTANDING WHO YOU ARE IS TO KNOW YOUR PURPOSE. IT'S ABOUT KNOWING YOUR **WHY**! FROM THE PREVIOUS EXERCISES, YOU SHOULD HAVE A PRETTY SOLID IDEA OF WHY YOU'RE SO FUCKING AWESOME, WHAT YOU'RE FIGHTING FOR AND WHAT YOU WANT YOUR LEGACY TO BE. THIS IS A KILLER TIME TO REFLECT ON THESE EXERCISES!

Write a 1-2 sentence purpose statement that explains specifically what you want to fight for, who you're helping and what you want the end result to be.

Examples:

- To help others live a healthy life at their peak fitness so that they can enjoy every moment of life in great health.

- To make the world a better place by helping superheroes everywhere discover their true powers.

Purpose Statement:

____

____

____

SUIT UP!
Grab those colorful pencils and markers - it's time to create your mighty superhero self!

Draw and name yourself as the superhuman you are. Bedazzle your outfit however you want! That includes hairstyle, a mask, a cape, and anything else that reflects your sexy self! Have fun and don't worry about being a Picasso here.

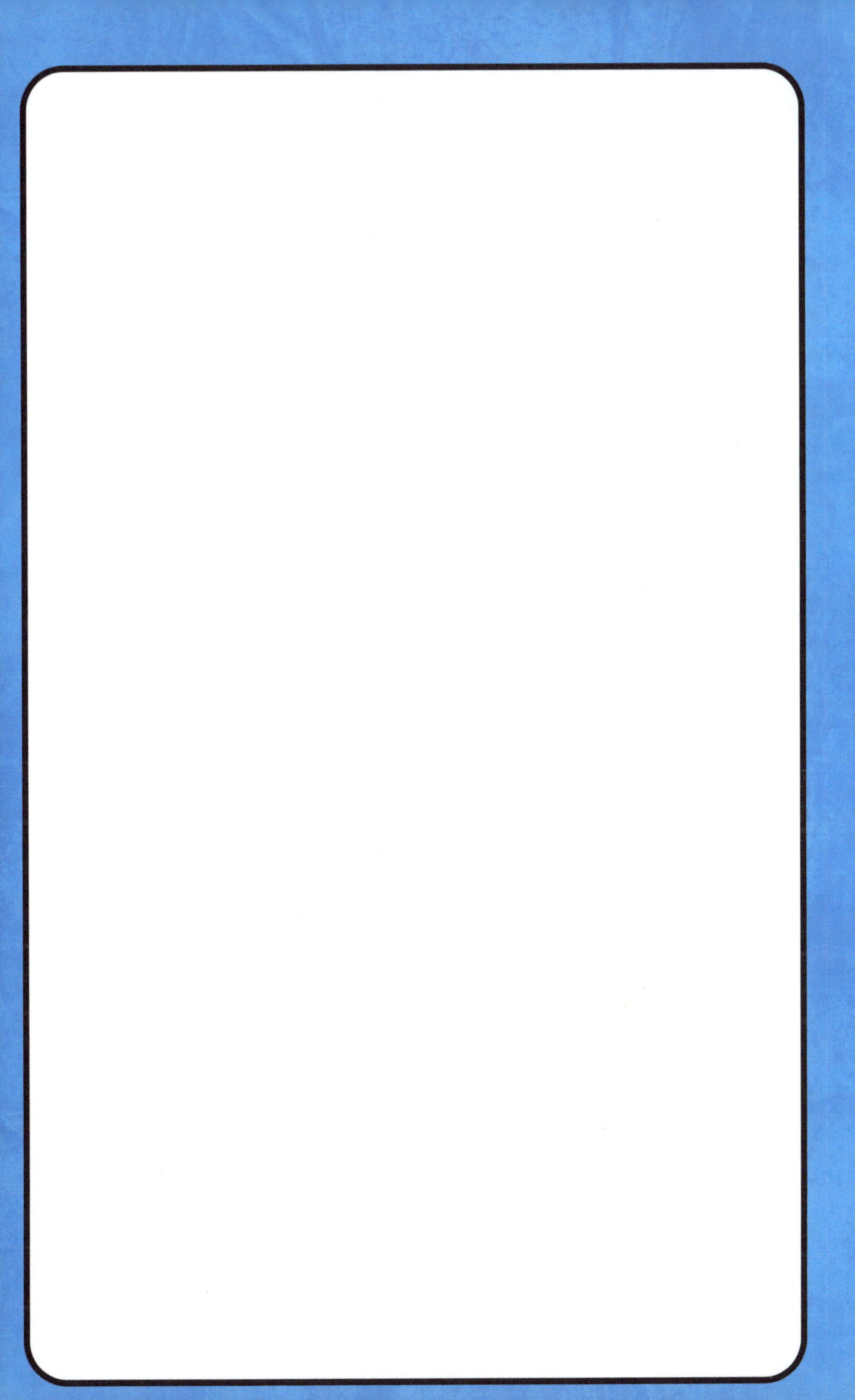

COMBAT TRAINING:
Kick the shit outta fear, limiting beliefs, and negative self-talk
CH 2
Fuck
FEAR
Fuck Everything And Run or
Face Everything And Rise

IT'S NO SECRET THAT OUR BUSY LIFESTYLES AND SHITTY HEALTH CHOICES CAN KNOCK US ON OUR ASSES. WHAT MATTERS MOST IS THAT WE GIVE OUR HEADS A SHAKE AND KEEP GETTING BACK UP TO FIGHT FOR OURSELVES. NO MATTER WHERE YOU'RE AT, IT'S NEVER TOO LATE TO TAKE CONTROL OF YOUR HEALTH AND GET BACK ON TRACK. COLOR IN YOUR HEALTH LEVELS BELOW, BASED ON THESE REFERENCE EXAMPLES:

Full: You're **KILLING IT** in this area and are operating at peak levels!

Halfsies: You've got some things going well here but still need to pick up the slack, Jack!

Near empty: Dude, you're fucked in this area right now! Your health is failing – get your ass in gear to get back on track!

WHERE ARE YOUR HEALTH LEVELS AT?

Fitness		**Career**
Diet		**Spiritual**
Mental		**Personal Growth**
Relationships		**Environmental**

(Effect of your daily habits on the environment)

Where do you most need to pull up your socks and make some positive changes?

____

What are 3 ways you can start making improvements with your health levels today?

____

____

____

____

Know Thy Enemy

Everyone has to deal with villains at some point in their life. Negativity, fear, shame, anxiety, and procrastination are just a handful of these good-for-nothing scumbags.

	Perfectatron	Boiling Point	The Procrastinaut
DESCRIPTION	A robot that is hardwired to execute all things perfectly, expect perfection from others and to be perfect themself.	Testy AF. Always a moment away from reaching their boiling point and exploding with rage and anger.	With their head in outer-space, they live in their own little world of make-believe, free of drive and accountability.
EVIL POWERS	Gives you worry warts as it always wants you to agonize about failure.	Super destructive when angry, they burn everything in their warpath.	Will tempt you to float through life with ease, leaving your goals and ambitions behind for another day.
HOW TO SLAY	Fearlessly fail really hard so they see that failure ain't as bad as they think it is.	A compassionate, listening ear is often more well-received than reactively barking advice or getting pissy yourself.	Pull them back down to Earth and get them focused on one damn thing at a time!

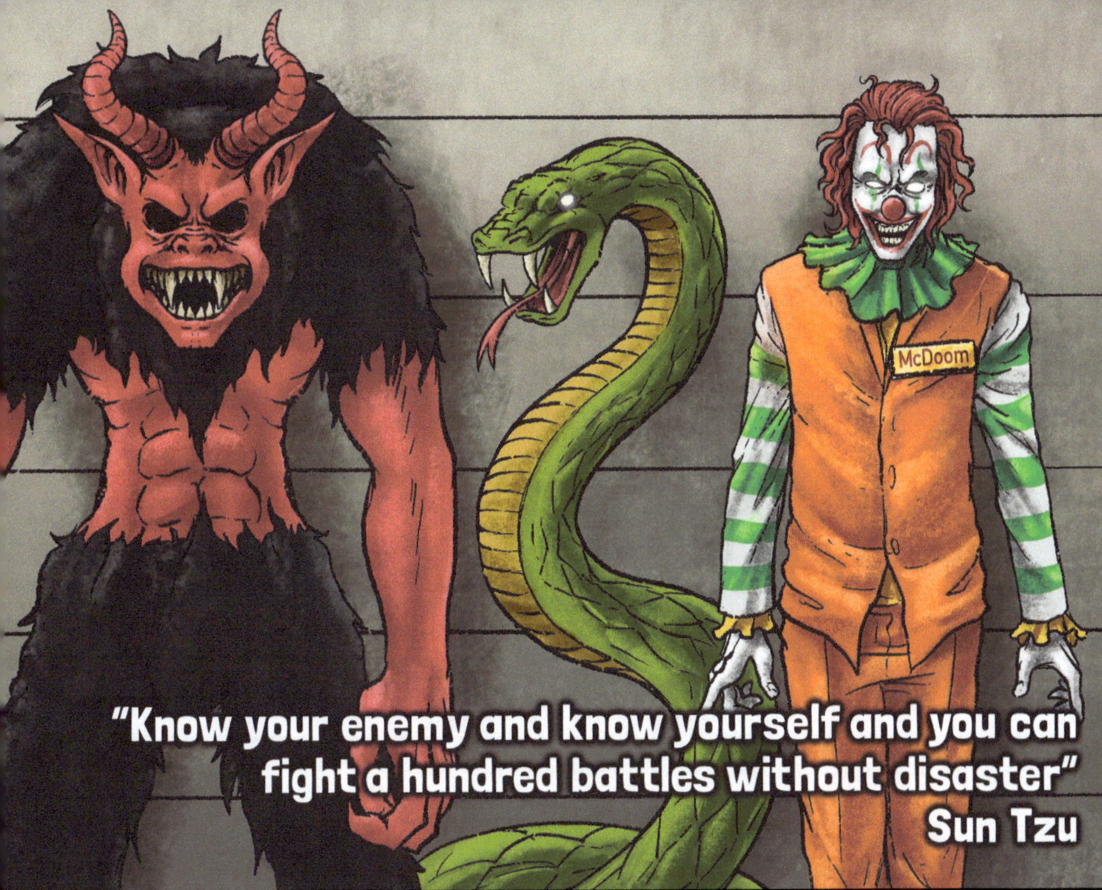

If you so desire to drop-kick their asses, you must know them better than they know themselves. Which of the villains below have tried to torment you in the past?

Fear Monster

A lying, overdramatic beast that corrupts your mind, obliterates all reasoning, and tears apart your hopes and dreams.

Infects the part of your brain responsible for rational thinking and decision making with fear, anxiety and analysis paralysis.

Do the thing that the monster thinks is scary! By confronting fear face-to-face, your Fear Monster will shut the hell up.

Shame Snake

A shady reptile that thrives on making you feel ashamed and worthless.

Slithers into your consciousness right before you go to sleep to remind you of something lame you did 7 years ago.

Yell "Get this motherfucking snake out of my motherfucking brain!" (Credit to Samuel L. Jackson)

Gloom McDoom

A pessimistic poop through and through, does nothing but spread doom, gloom and fake news.

Spews fear about the future, and sucks all the life and hope out of you.

Let that negativity bounce off of you like a dodgeball to a kid's face.

THE VILLAINS IN YOUR LIFE

NOW THAT YOU'VE MET SOME OF THE JERKS THAT SABOTAGE THE MINDS OF SO MANY PEOPLE AROUND THE WORLD, IT'S TIME TO STRATEGIZE HOW WE'LL DEFEAT ALL OF THE VILLAINS IN YOUR LIFE.

HOW TO DISCOVER THE VILLAINS IN YOUR LIFE: Think about personal behaviors, emotions, destructive thinking patterns, or negative influences around you. What in your mind is continually holding you back or knocking you down? Feel free to reference any of the villains from **'Know Thy Enemy'**.

WHAT ARE THEIR EVIL POWERS? Think about how each of these villains affect you.

HOW TO DEFEAT: Throw down some bullet points on how you can begin to fight them so the next time they come around you're ready to rumble.

Villain Name	Evil Powers	How to Defeat

WHAT DISTRACTING AND NEGATIVE CRAP CONSTANTLY MAKES YOU FEEL LIKE A BIG BAG OF DICKS? AIN'T NOBODY GOT TIME FOR THAT! THE SOONER YOU ACKNOWLEDGE THE CRAP, THE SOONER YOU CAN TELL IT TO **GET THE FUCK OUTTA HERE!** (SAYING WITH AN ITALIAN ACCENT HIGHLY ENCOURAGED)

SOMETIMES YOU JUST GOTTA MAKE LIKE ELSA AND LET THAT SHIT GO!

Get the fuck outta here negative self-talk!

Get the fuck outta here toxic relationship!

YOUR TURN! Write as many as you like. Saying them out loud really helps!

Get the fuck outta here

Get the fuck outta here

Get the fuck outta here

Get the fuck outta here

Get the fuck outta here

Get the fuck outta here

Get the fuck outta here

Get the fuck outta here

Get the fuck outta here

THE ART OF NOTICING SHIT

MANY SUPERHEROES HAVE ENHANCED SENSES LIKE X-RAY VISION, SUPER-HEARING, OR ABILITIES THAT HELP THEM DETECT WHEN SOMETHING BAD WILL HAPPEN NEARBY. YOU PROBABLY WON'T BE ABLE TO DEVELOP X-RAY VISION (UNLESS YOU DRINK TOO MUCH MOUNTAIN DEW) BUT THERE ARE OTHER WAYS YOU CAN DEVELOP YOUR SUPER SENSES.

THE MIND IS A FREAKING POWERFUL SOURCE OF SUPERHUMAN CAPABILITY. UNFORTUNATELY, WE CONSTANTLY NUMB OUR SENSES BY PICKING UP OUR DEVICES AT THE INSTANT WE FIND OURSELVES GETTING BORED OR HAVE FALLEN TEN MINUTES BEHIND ON OUR SOCIAL MEDIA FEEDS (GOOD HEAVENS, NO!).

TRAINING YOUR MIND TO TAP INTO ALL YOUR SENSES IN THE PRESENT MOMENT IS THE SUBTLE ART OF NOTICING SHIT. BY SIMPLY TAKING A FEW MOMENTS IN YOUR DAY TO OBSERVE THE FINE-ASS DETAIL OF A SPRING FLOWER, THE DUSTY CLUMPS OF YOUR GF'S HAIR IN YOUR CARPET, OR THE CHEESY GOODNESS OF A MOUNTAIN OF NACHOS, YOU'RE TRAINING YOUR MIND TO BE SUPER SENSE-ITIVE.

Take a minute right now to admire some fucking beauty and feel some gratitude for the simple things in your nearby surroundings...

I love carpet... I love desk... I love lamp... I love...

I love	I love	I love
I love	I love	I love
I love	I love	I love

OPTIMUS PRIMING

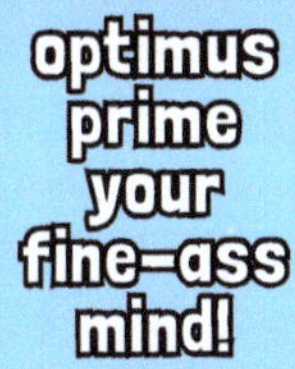

BEFORE YOU PAINT A WALL, YOU NEED TO USE A PRIMER COAT FIRST. WHY? TO PREPARE IT FOR THE SNAZZY PAINT JOB THAT COMES AFTER IT. THE SAME APPLIES TO THE START OF YOUR DAY. IF YOU WANT TO ACCOMPLISH SHIT AND FEEL GREAT, YOU FIRST NEED TO...

THE GOAL OF PRIMING IS TO MENTALLY SHIFT YOUR ASS INTO THE RIGHT GEAR FIRST THING IN THE MORNING. INSTEAD OF DOING THE "ROLL AND SCROLL" UPON OPENING YOUR CRUSTY EYES, MAKE THOSE FIRST THOUGHTS AND FEELINGS IN YOUR BRAIN POSITIVELY FUCKING BEAUTIFUL WITH THIS MINDFULNESS EXERCISE.

1. Get comfortable by either lying down in bed or sitting up.

2. Close your eyes and breathe in and out to the count of 10, focusing only on the sound or feeling of your breath.

3. Think of 3 moments you're grateful for. Vividly picture them as if you're there once again and notice how you feel. Feel the sensation of gratitude throughout your body for these moments or the people in them.

____

____

____

4. Return to focusing on your breathe once more to the count of 10.

5. Now, visualize 3 moments you're going to create in your day today. Think about how your positive attitude will energize others around you. Think about how you're going to kick ass today at your job. Visualize how it feels to put a smile on the face of someone that's important to you.

____

____

____

6. Finally, open your eyes, place your feet on the ground and repeat a short statement that pumps you up, like: 'I am fucking awesome', 'today is my day' or 'let's do this shit'.

____

Find Your FIGHT CLUB

MOVING YOUR BODY MOVES THE MIND. NO MATTER HOW IN OR OUT OF SHAPE YOU ARE, THERE'S ALWAYS SOMETHING YOU CAN DO TO GET THAT BIG 'OL HEART OF YOURS PUMPING! EXERCISE HAS COUNTLESS HEALTH BENEFITS AND ONE OF THE MOST IMPORTANT ONES IS HOW IT BENEFITS YOUR MENTAL HEALTH.

PHYSICAL ACTIVITY GIFTS YOUR BRAIN WITH THESE FUCKING WONDERFUL THINGS CALLED ENDORPHINS THAT MAKE YOU FEEL GOOD! YOU DO WANT TO FEEL GOOD, RIGHT?!

Think big but start small – what are some routines that you can slide into your daily/weekly schedule? Think about sports or activities that you actually enjoy doing, or have always wanted to try. Depending on your physical abilities, some great places to start are walking, saving cats from trees, yoga, pole dancing, or joining a **FIGHT CLUB!** (But do not talk about fight club). Plan out your next 2 weeks here:

EXERCISE	TIME OF DAY	DAY OF THE WEEK

WATCH YOUR FUCKING LANGUAGE

IT'S EASY AS PIE TO POINT OUT THE ALWAYS-COMPLAINING ENERGY ZOMBIES IN OUR LIVES, ISN'T IT? IT'S DRAINING TO BE AROUND PEOPLE WHO ARE CONSTANTLY BITCHING ABOUT THEIR PROBLEMS AND WHAT'S WRONG WITH EVERYTHING AND EVERYONE. BUT DO YOU EVER NOTICE WHEN **YOU'RE** BEING THE **ENERGY ZOMBIE**?

BECOMING AWARE OF YOUR OWN VERBAL DIARRHEA IS THE START OF TRANSFORMING THE QUALITY OF THE WORDS YOU SPEAK. DO YOU WANT TO LEAVE THOSE AROUND YOU FEELING RATTLED, HEAVY, AND DEPLETED? OR WOULD YOU RATHER LEAVE PEOPLE FEELING LIGHT, UPLIFTED, AND INSPIRED? THAT'S WHAT I THOUGHT, YOU RAY OF FUCKING SUNSHINE!

ENERGY ZOMBIES

People who drain the life out of a room with their need to feed off of negativity.

Write down some situations that turn you into a monster. Do you lash out in anger when someone doesn't agree with you? Do you berate others when they make mistakes? Are you constantly complaining about shit? Note how you typically react to these situations, and then come up with a more positive, rational, and compassionate response for next time. Practice catching yourself in the moment right away, take a few deep breaths and just watch your fucking language next time.

SITUATION	TYPICAL REACTION	BETTER WAY TO REACT

COME TO THE LOVE SIDE

HUMAN BEINGS ARE UNCONSCIOUSLY AND TOTALLY WHIPPED BY THEIR EMOTIONS. WHETHER YOU KNOW IT OR NOT, THE EMOTIONS YOU FEEL EVERYDAY FALL EITHER ON THE 'LOVE SIDE' OR THE 'FEAR SIDE'.

IN SIMPLE TERMS, THE WAY YOU FEEL IS BASED ON THE MEANING YOU GIVE TO THINGS. FOR EXAMPLE, IF IT'S POURING RAIN OUTSIDE YOUR MIND MAY BE LINKED UP TO THE PATTERN THAT YOU ALWAYS FEEL SAD AND LETHARGIC (FEAR SIDE) ON THESE TYPES OF DAYS. IN ORDER TO CHANGE THAT BULLSHIT REACTION, YOU NEED TO:

1. **RECOGNIZE THE MEANING AND EMOTION:** Make a conscious effort to recognize the meaning that you're giving to the rainy day and the resulting crap emotion.

2. **INTERRUPT THAT BS PATTERN:** Consciously link up a new, more positive meaning to this type of weather such as, "Rainy days are lovely because they're refreshing and make everything smell fucking delightful!" (Love Side).

3. **CREATE A HAPPY HABIT:** It takes more than one time to change your old BS thought patterns – you gotta keep watering that positive emotion for several months until it's just a natural habit.

The Meaning You Give Things = The Emotions You Feel

The Emotions You Feel = How You Perceive Your Life

1. Write down all the typical emotions you feel on a daily basis – the good, bad and the ugly.

2. Circle two positive and two negative emotions that you feel most often.

3. Write down what typically triggers these four emotions.

4. Write down positive new meanings you can give to the 2 BS emotions.

Challenge: Review these for the next 14 days. Try keeping a tab of how many times you catch yourself in a negative thought pattern. Aim to reduce that crap every day. Did you improve by Day 14?

1	2	3	4	5	6	7

8	9	10	11	12	13	14

Drop Kick Your Limiting Beliefs

I'm too old. I just don't have the time. I'll always be single. I don't have the education or skills for that. I'm no expert. Things never go my way.

THAT HURT TO WRITE. Please do me a favor and scribble out, tear, burn all that crap written above or wipe your ass with it.

Shit happens in life that leads us to form these BS thought patterns. They're usually caused by past experiences or from believing the opinions of a small percentage of dickheads in our surrounding cultures. Everyone goes through having limiting beliefs, but the key to rising above them is training yourself on how to quickly notice them and drop kick 'em into oblivion.

STEP 1: Identify the limiting belief. Call it out and get yourself ready to throw down.

STEP 2: What situation(s) or people caused this limiting belief to form?

STEP 3: What will happen if you continue to let this limiting belief beat you down?

STEP 4: Replace your limiting belief with all kinds of positive facts and reinforcing affirmations that pump you up for the daily fight.

If someone else has done it then it's possible. Heck, even if no one has done it, there are millions of examples of humans doing what was thought to be impossible.

Step 1: LIMITING BELIEF #1: ____

____

Step 2: CAUSE	Step 3: LEVERAGE	Step 4: THE FACTS

Step 1: LIMITING BELIEF #2: ____

____

Step 2: CAUSE	Step 3: LEVERAGE	Step 4: THE FACTS

Step 1: LIMITING BELIEF #3: ____

____

Step 2: CAUSE	Step 3: LEVERAGE	Step 4: THE FACTS

YOU ARE WHAT YOU EAT

THE MATHEMATICS ARE PRETTY SIMPLE: EAT GARBAGE, FEEL LIKE GARBAGE. EAT HEALTHY, FEEL HEALTHY! WHAT A CONCEPT! WHAT YOU FUEL YOUR BODY WITH MAKES A HUGE DIFFERENCE IN HOW MUCH ASS-KICKING YOU CAN DO.

THERE AIN'T NOTHING SUPER ABOUT EATING LIKE CRAP. WHEN YOUR BODY IS LACKING NUTRIENTS AND OVERLOADED WITH SUGAR, CAFFEINE, SALT, ALCOHOL, ETC., IS IT ANY WONDER THAT YOU WOULD FEEL LIKE SHIT ALL THE TIME? YOUR DIET ALSO AFFECTS NOT ONLY JUST YOUR PHYSICAL HEALTH, BUT YOUR BRAIN HEALTH TOO! NUTRIENT DEFICIENCY CAN CAUSE FEELINGS OF ANXIETY, DEPRESSION, SHIT-FOR-BRAINS, EXHAUSTION, LETHARGY, AND MORE.

SO, WHAT IS A SUPERHUMAN TO DO? IF YOU WANT TO START MAKING HEALTHY CHANGES IN HOW YOU EAT, THE KEY IS TO START SMALL! JUST LIKE ROME WASN'T BUILT IN A DAY, NEITHER CAN YOU OVERHAUL YOUR DIET IN A DAY. THINK OF THE FOOD GROUPS YOU'RE LACKING IN, AND THE ONES THAT YOU MAYBE LOVE A LITTLE TOO MUCH. WHAT MEALS ARE YOU THE MOST LAZY ABOUT?

Challenge yourself to find two healthy recipes that can replace your not-so-healthy ones. Make your shopping list here and snap a photo of it to take with you to the grocery store!

FEEL GOOD GROCERY LIST

FROM TIME TO TIME, WE ALL FACE THOSE BIG 'OL SHITTY EMOTIONS LIKE ANGER, ANXIETY AND SADNESS. JUST LIKE YOU SHOULDN'T STARE DIRECTLY AT THE BLAZING SUN FOR TOO LONG, YOU SHOULDN'T HANG OUT WITH YOUR SUCKY EMOTIONS FOR TOO LONG.

MAKE YOURSELF A LI'L LIST OF SOME SOOTHING AND CONSTRUCTIVE THINGS YOU CAN DO TO FEEL BETTER IN ANY MOMENT.

SOME GOOD EXAMPLES: TAKE A FEW DEEP BREATHS, MEDITATE, GO FOR A WALK, WRITE IN YOUR JOURNAL, CALL A SIDEKICK, HAVE A CUP OF TEA, PUNCH AN INANIMATE OBJECT, OR SCREAM INTO YOUR PILLOW.

Haters Gonna Hate, Potatoes Gonna Potate

NO MATTER HOW FUCKING LOVELY OF A PERSON YOU ARE, AT SOME POINT IN LIFE YOU'RE GONNA HAVE HATER POTATERS. THE MORE SUCCESSFUL YOU BECOME, THE MORE YOU'LL LIKELY ATTRACT THOSE TATERS.

HAS ANYONE EVER TOLD YOU THAT YOU COULDN'T DO SOMETHING BECAUSE YOU'RE TOO ________AND NOT ENOUGH ___________?

FUCK THAT!

Reframe those criticisms and let them become your **FUEL!** List some bullshit criticisms you've received in your life and how you can positively reframe them to make 'em your jet fuel!

____

____

____

____

____

____

____

____

____

____

____

____

Roast those goddamn hater potaters and chow down on success!

REWRITING YOUR ORIGIN STORY

YOU AND EVERYONE ON THE PLANET HAVE BEEN THROUGH SOME VARIETY OF HEAVY SHIT. SOME HIDE IT BETTER THAN OTHERS AND SOME WEAR IT ON THEIR SLEEVES.

IT'S EASY TO SPEND YEARS BEING DEPRESSED ABOUT THE LIMITATIONS IN YOUR LIFE OR WHAT HAS HAPPENED TO YOU. IT'S ALSO REALLY FUCKING HARD. BEING STUCK IN THE PAST ROBS YOU OF YOUR POWERS AND BLINDS YOU TO THE POSSIBILITIES OF TOMORROW.

"One day, in retrospect, the years of struggle will strike you as the most beautiful." - Sigmund Freud

YOU CAN'T CHANGE YOUR PAST, BUT YOU CAN CHANGE THE STORY YOU TELL YOURSELF TODAY. YOU ARE ALIVE AT THIS VERY MOMENT FOR A FUCKING REASON!

Stop focusing on your disabilities and be grateful for your amazing **ABILITIES**.

Stop letting the fear of failure paralyze you and **BRAVELY** chase the shit out of your dreams.

Stop seeking sympathy from others and start showing them how goddamn **STRONG** you are.

Stop making **EXCUSES** and start making shit happen!

CRITICAL CHALLENGES

List a few critical moments (challenges, traumas or heartbreaks) from your past that are often in the back of your mind, or ones you are dealing with daily.

POWERFUL NEW STORY

Write down how these situations make you a stronger superhuman or how you're moving forward from them. Write your powerful new story below that can inspire others who may be facing similar challenges.

CH 3

Create Your Epic HQ
"Our environment, the world in which we live and work,
is a mirror of our attitude and expectations."
- Earl Nightingale

TIDY YOUR HIDEY-HOLE

YOU KNOW WHAT THEY SAY: CLUTTERED SPACE, CLUTTERED MIND.

WHETHER YOUR HQ IS AN APARTMENT, YOUR BEDROOM OR A CARDBOARD BOX, ALL SUPERHUMANS LIKE YOU NEED AN ORGANIZED, FUNCTIONAL PLACE WHERE THEY CAN LIVE THEIR BEST LIFE. DOES YOUR HIDEY-HOLE GIVE YOU SATISFYING FEELINGS OF COMFORT AND PEACE, OR DOES IT MAKE YOU WANT TO LIGHT THE PLACE ON FIRE?

It's time to make your space operate at its best and feel like the ultimate superhero headquarters. What are the most problematic areas of your HQ that need some TLC in the clutter department? List all the areas you're going to tidy the ef up!

The Panic Room

<table>
<tr>
<td>

DO YOU HAVE THE ATTENTION SPAN OF A GNAT? ARE YOU UNABLE TO ESCAPE THE ENDLESS PINGS AND DINGS BLOWING UP YOUR PHONE EVERY WAKING MINUTE OF THE DAY? ARE YOU COMPLETELY OVERWHELMED BY EVERY FUCKING PERSON IN YOUR LIFE CLAWING FOR YOUR ATTENTION AND ALL YOU WANT IS A SINGLE GODDAMN MOMENT OF PEACE?

</td>
<td>

Then you need a PANIC ROOM!

</td>
</tr>
</table>

Where in your space can you relax or get a ton of creative work completed with no one harassing you? Does this place even exist for you?

____

Jot down some ideas on how you could create or improve this space in your world.

____

____

____

____

____

What distractions do you need to do a better job of removing?

____

____

____

____

____

____

The Weapons Room

IF YOU WANT TO BE PREPARED FOR WHATEVER LIFE THROWS YOUR WAY, YOU'VE GOT TO HAVE A KICK-ASS ARSENAL OF WEAPONS TO CHOOSE FROM! CHECK OFF WHICH ONES YOU NEED MOST:

CORPORATE LADDER

Stretch out those legs and climb your way to the top of any powerful organization with this handy packable ladder.

BULLSHIT DEFLECTOR

Hold close this solid hunk of NOPE and protect yourself from getting people's bullshit all over you. Blissfully watch that BS slide right off like water off a duck's back.

SEX MAGNET

Whip out this rod and attract the right kind of people into your life, and pants.

EXTRA ABSORPTION ADULT DIAPERS

For when fear hits you right in the bowels. No one likes poopy-filled spandex.

POSITIVI-WHIP

Debbie Downers be gone! Whip 'em with some positivity. Whip 'em real good.

FEAR-FUCKING BLASTERS

Flip fear the bird and blast it into oblivion with this almost-too-much-fun toy.

TRUTH BOMBS

Sometimes people need to hear the cold, hard truth. Toss one of these at 'em and watch it emit a hot blast of accountability.

SUPER SIMPLIFICATION SHIT-O-METER

Place overly complicated shit into the Shit-O-Meter and it'll simplify the shit out of it for you.

CHILL-OUT SURFBOARD

Float on and let the cool caress of this surfboard instantly calm your shit.

What other gear or tools do you need to help you haul ass and fight for your dreams? For example: If your dream is to be a successful photographer, you'll need some dope-ass camera equipment, etc. Think big and make a list here:

____

____

____

____

____

____

____

____

____

Reading Makes My Brain Hurt
SIDEKICKd
Man's Search for His Socks
by Victor Coldankles
THE 4 HOUR DUMP
Think and Grow Weed
By Napoleon Chill
The Power of Wow
by Owen Wilson
Awaken The Butterfly Within
The Art of Day Drinking
ZEN RABBITS
How to Lose Friends and Scare People
The Life Changing Magic of Tidying Yo Shit Up

IF YOU WANT TO BECOME THE BEST AT A CERTAIN SKILL, IT'LL TAKE A LOT OF PRACTICE, READING AND LEARNING FROM THE VERY BEST.

BURN YOUR ALGEBRA BOOKS AND BUILD YOUR EPIC LIBRARY OF KNOWLEDGE WITH SOME GOOD SHIT YOU ACTUALLY CARE ABOUT. CONTINUALLY LEARNING SCARES THE ZOMBIES OUT OF THE CORNERS OF YOUR MIND; BECAUSE IF YOU'RE NOT GROWING YOU'RE ROTTING LIKE ONE OF THEM.

What are some skills or areas in your life that you want to take to the next level?

____

____

____

____

____

____

____

____

Take some time to research books that you can add to your bookshelf, YouTube channels you can subscribe to, or blogs you can follow (*ahem* like bravebud. com) that relate to your above list of skills.

____

____

____

____

____

____

THE LAUNCHPAD

Whether you're a car junkie or not, there's one badass killing-machine here that best represents one of the four human personality types in you. Are you an independent, fire-powered thrasher? Or are you a group-minded, flower-powered hunk of burning love?

As you read on, think about which one best reflects your awesomeness (and perhaps your saltiness, too). While you could feel like a mix of two, you'll probably have one that slaps you across the face a little harder.

When you understand what drives (pun intended!) yourself and others, you can figure out the best way to talk to, inspire and build trust with them. Awareness of yourself and others is fucking badass! Go wild and color in your launchpad!

Which personality type are you?

ROCKET SUIT (INDEPENDENT ADVENTURER)

Specs: Fast-mover, strikes quickly. Independent AF, demands freedom on tasks. Outgoing, large and in charge. Makes swift maneuvers to dodge by obstacles, silky smooth under high-stress situations.

Defects: Impatient, short-fused, makes abrupt decisions without consulting others.

Fuel: Independence. Unique challenges. Directness, urgency. High-reward/risk situations.

Turn-offs: Touchy-feely situations, emotions. Long-ass explanations.

SUPERCAR (FUN-LOVER)

Specs: Fast-paced, extroverted. Loves to have fun, enjoys getting noticed by people. Self-confident, charismatic.

Defects: Self-indulgent. Attention span of a fruit fly, impatient as hell. Egotistical. Total procrastinaut, doesn't finish off projects.

Fuel: Public recognition, being approved of. Succeeding ahead of close peers, being a trendsetter.

Turn-offs: Public humiliation. Being seen as unsuccessful, not being recognized.

TANK (ANALYZER)

Specs: Introverted. Meticulous, analytical, strategic. Crystal clear on direction. Packs a big-ass, accurate punch when ready to fire.

Defects: Slow as a sloth, takes longer to make decisions. Not a people pleaser.

Fuel: Controlled situations. Problem solving. Any chance to provide detailed analytics.

Turn-offs: Being rushed. Disorganization. Messy emotions.

HIPPIE VAN (PEACEMAKER)

Specs: Chill AF, fun to be around, makes everyone feel comfortable. Creative. Supportive of others and cares about their thoughts, opinions and buy-in to decisions.

Defects: Gets walked all over like a doormat, goes along with others' wants. Feels hurt easily. Shy, doesn't always share opinions.

Fuel: Calm, groovy environments. People pleasing. Having a damn good time with others.

Turn-offs: Pushy people. High-risk situations. Change from the norm routines.

HEROIC QUOTES

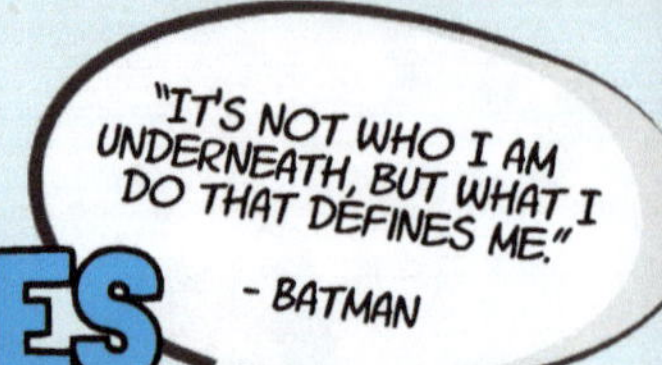

Everyday our headspace is inundated by the news, social media, and other BS. Therefore, surrounding yourself with motivational quotes, imagery, or anything that inspires you is a fucking splendid idea when sprucing up your HQ. It's always nice to be reminded of good shit, right?

Below are a few epic superhero quotes you could include in your space, or find your own that are meaningful to you!

"I THINK A HERO IS AN ORDINARY INDIVIDUAL WHO FINDS STRENGTH TO PERSEVERE AND ENDURE IN SPITE OF OVERWHELMING OBSTACLES."
- SUPERMAN

"WHEN LIFE GIVES YOU A BAG OF LEMONS, SQUEEZE THE FUCK OUT OF 'EM AND ENJOY YOUR LEMONADE."
- BRAVEBUD

"WHICH WILL HOLD GREATER RULE OVER YOU? YOUR FEAR OR YOUR CURIOSITY?"
- WONDER WOMAN

"IT'S NOT DYING THAT YOU NEED TO BE AFRAID OF, IT'S NEVER HAVING LIVED IN THE FIRST PLACE."
- THE GREEN HORNET

"HEROES ARE MADE BY THE PATH THEY CHOOSE, NOT THE POWERS THEY ARE GRACED WITH."
- IRON MAN

NOW IT'S YOUR TURN!
Find a few of your favorite quotes:

SUPER SLOGANS

Every superhero needs a slogan, catch phrase, or mantra – whatever you like to call it! It's a phrase or word that gets you fired up and motivated before you *take 'em to the cleaners.* (See what I did there?)

Learn from your favorite superheroes below:

"I AM THE VENGEANCE, I AM THE NIGHT, I AM BATMAN!" – **Batman**

The Incredible Hulk – "HULK SMASH!"

"MY SPIDEY SENSES ARE TINGLING" – **Spider-Man**

Wolverine – "I'M THE BEST THERE IS AT WHAT I DO."

"BALLS TO THE WALL POWER!" – **Bravebud**

IT'S TIME TO CREATE YOUR SUPER SLOGAN

1. A few tips: Less is more! Just a few words is all you need – profanity encouraged!
2. Does it get you pumped up and make you want to punch the air?
3. Is it related to who you are? Does it reflect your superpowers or what you're fucking awesome at? Think about a few words that represent the badass person you are:

World Domination Plan
CH 4

THE FUCKIT LIST

EVERYONE'S GOT A FEW BATSHIT CRAZY THINGS THEY WANT TO DO BEFORE THEY KICK THE BUCKET. LIFE IS SHORT: GIVE YOUR LIMITING BELIEFS A TALL GLASS OF STFU AND TELL 'EM **"Fuckit, I'm doing it!"**

YOU WANT TO OPEN A MOBILE HEDGEHOG GROOMING SALON?	**Fuckit, I'm doing it!**
BREAK A GUINNESS WORLD RECORD?	**Fuckit, I'm doing it!**
HIKE THE INCA TRAIL?	**Fuckit, I'm doing it!**

WHAT'S ON YOUR FUCKIT LIST?

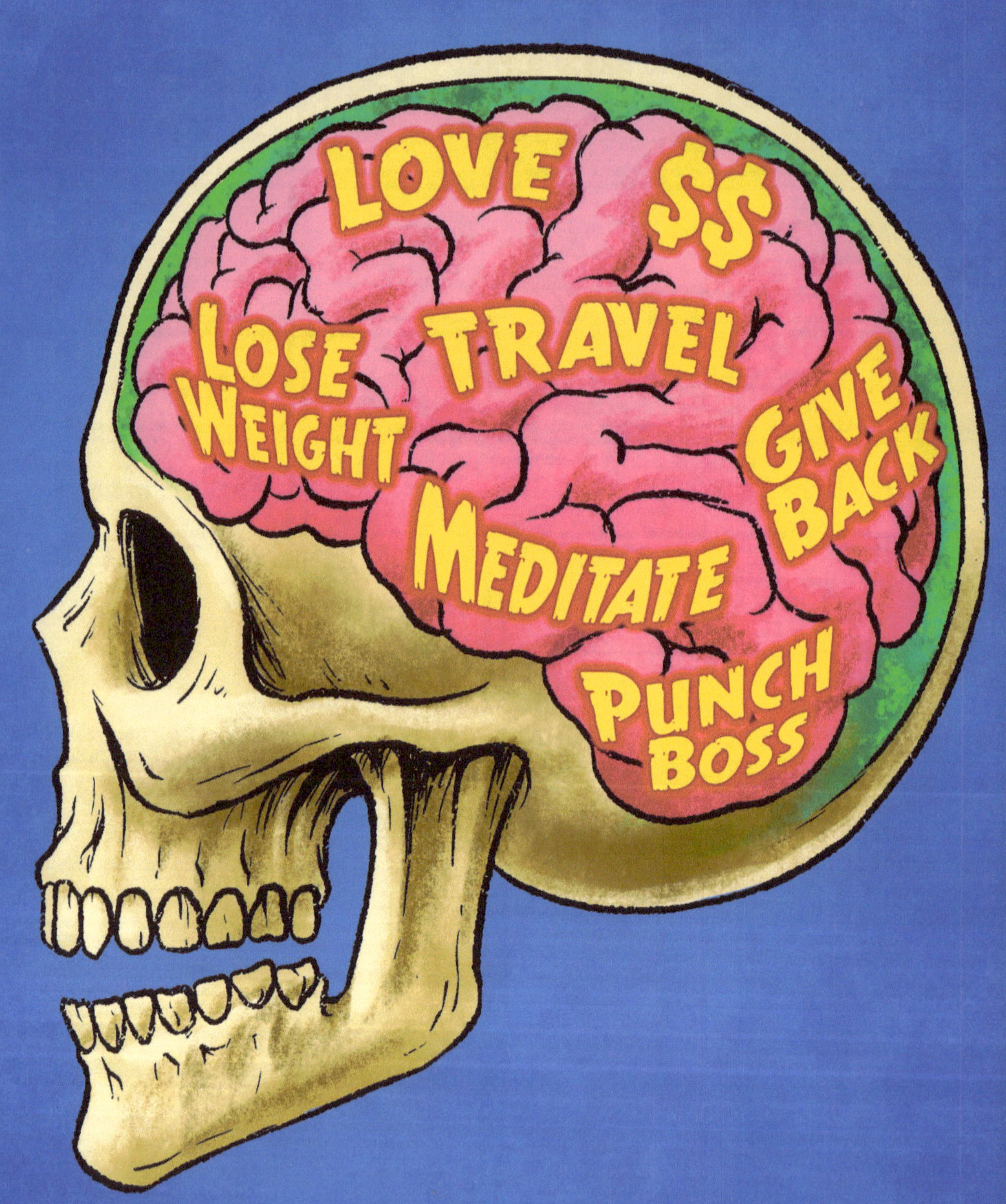

Keep Calm and Get Declusterfucked

DECLUSTERFUCKING

DO YOU EVER FEEL LIKE YOU'VE GOT TONS OF IDEAS BUT HAVE NO CLUE WHERE TO START? ENTER, DECLUSTERFUCKING: THE MAGICAL ART OF PULLING ALL THE JUMBLED UP THOUGHTS OUT OF YOUR BRAIN, DUMPING THEM OUT ON PAPER AND ORGANIZING THEM INTO HAPPY LITTLE CLUSTERS.

DREAM BIG AND WRITE DOWN EVERYTHING THAT POPS INTO YOUR HEAD WHEN ANSWERING THE QUESTIONS ON THE NEXT PAGES (FEEL FREE TO GRAB ANY OF YOUR IDEAS FROM THE FUCKIT LIST). DON'T JUDGE OR DOUBT WHAT YOU'RE WRITING, AND DON'T FUSS ABOUT MAKING EVERYTHING SOUND PEACHY PERFECT.

LEAVE THE 'MISSION CRITICAL RATING' COLUMN ALONE FOR NOW; WE'LL COME BACK TO THAT SECTION DURING A LATER EXERCISE.

HEALTH AND POWER LEVELS: How would you like to maintain or level up your health and diet? Think about exercises, changes to your diet, or activities for your uber-important mental health.

Ways I'd like to level up my health and diet...	MC Rating

FINANCIAL GAINZ: When you think about your financial situation, where would you like to be in the next year, 5 years, 10 years? What things would you like to be able to afford (house, car, butler, etc...)?

Where I see my financial situation in 1, 5, 10 years...	MC Rating

LEAGUE OF EXTRAORDINARY ASS-KICKING PEOPLE: How would you like to level up your relationships with friends, family, and lovers? Any relationships you'd like to strengthen or get out of? Also, think about new relationships you want in your life - mentors, coaches or trainers you'd like to add.

Ways I'd like to level up my relationships...	MC Rating

MAXIMUM EXCELLENCE: What are some achievements you'd like to knock off? Think about your career, side hustles, hobbies, or passion projects you'd like to do. What new skills would you like to learn (piano, painting, parkour, etc...)? Don't worry about planning out your whole life; just write whatever comes to mind. Whether your goal is for next month, year or decade, all are great!

Achievements in my life...	MC Rating

OTHERWORLDLINESS: In what ways would you like to make a difference in the lives of others? Are there any causes or charities you'd want to donate money, time or resources to? Think about all the ways you'd like to use your talents to bring some sunshine into peoples' lives.

How I'd like to add value to the lives of others...	MC Rating

CONGRATS! YOU JUST DECLUSTERFUCKED A BUNCH OF IMPORTANT SHIT THAT'S BEEN FLAILING AROUND IN YOUR HEAD. YOU'VE GROUPED ALL THESE AWESOME THOUGHTS INTO 5 VERY IMPORTANT CLUSTERS THAT, WITH THE RIGHT ROCKET FUEL, WILL TAKE YOU TO DIZZYING HEIGHTS YOU'VE NEVER IMAGINED!

MISSION CRITICALS

<table>
<tr>
<td>

Mission Criticals (MCs) are your absolutes, your musts, and your unwavering will-do's.

</td>
<td>

Go back through the Declusterfucking exercise and put a rating out of 4 in the 'Mission Critical Rating' column.

</td>
</tr>
</table>

4 = ABSO-FUCKIN-LUTELY: An absolute MUST. There's no way I'm waiting to pursue something this important!

3 = HECK YEAH: Definitely want to see this through, but right now I have bigger fish to fry.

2 = WOULD BE NICE: This sounds great, but it's not super critical to my success or happiness right now.

1 = MEH: Not a priority, and not really sure why I put this on my list.

Anything that you rate a 4 is 'Mission Critical'. These are the goals that are most crucial to your happiness and fulfillment in life. Ideally you should have 4-8 MCs. Heck, even 2 or 3 is fine as this will keep your focus narrowed in on what's most important to you. As you see progress, you can always move some of your 3's to 4's in the future to have more MCs.

Next, write out your MCs below and give them a simple name to remember them by. Examples – *Operation: 20lbs Down, Mission: Buy Car, Project: Punch Boss*

MC NAME	MISSION CRITICAL GOAL

Y Tho

McDonald's Employee Accused Of Smuggling 80 Lbs Of McNuggets In His Anal Cavity

Hooray! You've figured out some important shit you want to do! Y tho?

Ask yourself: Y is this so damn important to me? What do I have to lose if I don't make this shit happen? Who else will be affected if I don't? The more powerful your Y's become the more jet fuel you'll have to make them happen. (Hopefully they have nothing to do with McNuggets).

MC NAME	Y THO

BLAST OFF, MOTHERFUCKERS!

IT'S TIME TO LEARN HOW TO LAUNCH YOURSELF INTO THE PLAINS OF OTHERWORLDLINESS.

THE DECLUSTERFUCKING ROCKET OF HAPPINESS STRATEGICALLY ORGANIZES YOUR MISSION CRITICALS TO HELP PROPEL YOU TOWARDS A LIFE OF PURPOSE, FULFILLMENT AND SOMETHING PRETTY CLOSE TO HAPPINESS.

INPUT YOUR MCs INTO THE ROCKET ON THE RIGHT. START AT THE BOTTOM BY BUILDING A ROCK-SOLID FOUNDATION SUPPORTED BY TOP-NOTCH MENTAL, PHYSICAL AND EMOTIONAL HEALTH. THEN WORK YOUR WAY UP BUILDING THE REST OF THE ROCKET, EACH SECTION BEING JUST AS IMPORTANT AS THE PREVIOUS.

BUILDING AND LAUNCHING A ROCKET AIN'T NO EASY FEAT; IT TAKES HARD FUCKING WORK, FOCUS AND DETERMINATION. YOU DECIDE THE AMOUNT OF JET FUEL THAT GOES INTO IT AND HOW FAR IT WILL GO!

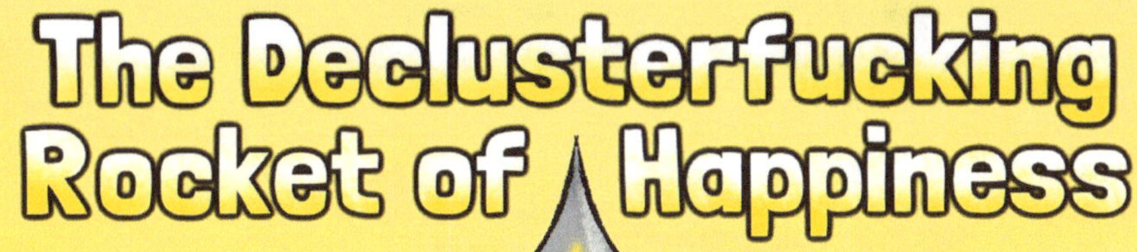

The Declusterfucking
Rocket of Happiness

OTHERWORLDLINESS
(Purpose fulfillment, contribution,
adding value to others)

MAXIMUM EXCELLENCE
(Career, passion project, achievements)

LEAGUE OF EXTRAORDINARY ASS-KICKING PEOPLE
(Important relationships)

FINANCIAL GAINZ
(Money, house, car, etc.)

HEALTH AND POWER LEVELS
(Physical, mental, emotional)

Grit
Willpower
Maximum Effort
Determination
purpose
passion

MILESTONING

Smashing your Mission Criticals into itty-bitty milestones is imperative to achieving your **happy endings** in life. Bite-sized pieces are easier to swallow than big gnarly chunks.

For your MCs you should have clear outcomes that you're trying to achieve by a set date such as **lose 10 lbs by [x date]** or **put away $30,000 in your savings by [y date] to be able to quit your lame-ass day job.**

When you look at these **happy endings** they're measurable and can therefore be easily broken down into shorter milestones.

EXAMPLE

MC NAME: *Operation: 20lbs Down*

Start Date
May 1

Milestone: 5lbs lost
Date: June 1

12lbs lost
Aug 1

20lbs lost
Oct 1

NOW IT'S YOUR TURN. Write down all of your MC Names and plot out as many milestones as you think are necessary to stay on track. Pick dates and milestones that are realistic and don't beat yourself up if you don't achieve one; just troubleshoot and course correct!

MC NAME:

MC NAME:

MC NAME:

MC NAME:

MC NAME:

MC NAME:

MC NAME:

CONGRATULATIONS! You've set up a kick-ass plan for getting some serious shit done. On the next page, we're going to layer in the most important ingredient to help you accomplish all of these great milestones.
REMEMBER: a plan doesn't mean shit if you don't put in the gusto to execute it.

HEROIC HABITS

YOU'VE PROBABLY HEARD OF THAT BULLSHIT STATISTIC THAT SAYS MOST PEOPLE GIVE UP ON THEIR NEW YEAR'S RESOLUTIONS JUST THREE WEEKS INTO THE YEAR. YOU'RE INITIALLY ALL FIRED UP ABOUT YOUR GOAL, THEN HIT YOUR FIRST LITTLE SETBACK, AND DECIDE TO GIVE UP LIKE A TOTAL WUSSY.

SUPERHEROES IN TRAINING FACE THE SAME PROBLEM: ONE MOMENT YOU'RE LEARNING TO JUMP FROM BUILDING TO BUILDING, THE NEXT, GRAVITY HAS YOU HURDLING EARTHBOUND INTO A DUMPSTER. HOW DO YOU GET MOTIVATED TO CRAWL OUTTA THE DUMPSTER, PEEL THE DEAD CAT OFF YOUR HEAD AND BOUNCE BACK WITH MORE ENERGY THAN BEFORE? IT'S SIMPLE: GET YOURSELF SOME **HEROIC HABITS**.

THESE HABITS ARE THE SECRET SAUCE TO ULTIMATELY ACHIEVING YOUR MISSION CRITICALS! ANYONE CAN PROGRAM GOOD HABITS INTO THEIR BRAINS BY SETTING UP THE RIGHT ROUTINE LOOP TO AUTOMATICALLY TRIGGER EACH ONE.

Routine loop = Firestarter, Habit and Rewardgasm

In the table on the right complete the following:

1. **HABITS:** Research the daily habits of successful superhumans who share similar MCs to yours (*example: Google search 'how does Scarlett Johansson get in shape for a movie?'*). Pick the ones that could work for you. Your habits are the 'how' you're gonna make your MC happen. You may have 1 of these or in some cases you may have 7,10, or 15.

2. **FIRESTARTERS:** Write down the cues/triggers you can set in place to automatically remind yourself to complete each habit (*examples: putting your workout gear at the end of your bed for the next morning's workout, setting a reminder in your phone, playing a song that pumps you up*).

3. **REWARDGASMS:** Write down the rewards that would actually turn you on, and give you a big 'gasm' to complete these habits every day (*examples: working out = an afternoon nap, or a special cheat meal once a week*).

On average it takes at least 21 days to develop a habit and 90 days to make it a lifestyle change.

So don't fucking give up after 21 days!

MC NAME:

HABITS	FIRESTARTERS	REWARDGASMS

MC NAME:

HABITS	FIRESTARTERS	REWARDGASMS

MC NAME:

HABITS	FIRESTARTERS	REWARDGASMS

MC NAME:

HABITS	FIRESTARTERS	REWARDGASMS

MC NAME:

HABITS	FIRESTARTERS	REWARDGASMS

MC NAME:

HABITS	FIRESTARTERS	REWARDGASMS

MC NAME:

HABITS	FIRESTARTERS	REWARDGASMS

MC NAME:

HABITS	FIRESTARTERS	REWARDGASMS

THE NEXT STEP TO KICKING ASS WITH YOUR HABITS AND ACTUALLY COMPLETING THEM ON THE DAILY IS TO PLAN OUT SPECIFIC DAYS AND TIMES TO EXECUTE THEM. WHEN YOU GET TO CHAPTER 6 WE'LL WORK ON DEVELOPING SOME OF YOUR ROUTINES FOR GETTING SHIT DONE.

IF YOU'RE ON A HEROIC HABITS HIGH AND WANT TO KEEP GOING, YOU CAN SKIP OVER TO CH. 6 AND COMPLETE 'LET'S GET SHIT DONE'.

The Crazy Wall

DID YOU KNOW THAT A **CRAZY WALL** IS THAT THING THAT INVESTIGATORS AND SUPERHEROES USE TO ORGANIZE PICTURES OF ALL THE EVIDENCE THEY HAVE FOR A CASE? ALL GREAT INVESTIGATORS SET UP A CRAZY WALL TO BREAK DOWN ALL THE SMALL CLUES TO FIGURE OUT HOW TO SOLVE THEIR CASE.

SIMILARLY, HAVING AN INSPIRATIONAL WALL THAT YOU SEE EVERY DAY WITH THE HAPPY ENDINGS YOU WANT TO ACHIEVE ACTS AS A CONTINUAL REMINDER OF WHAT YOU'RE WORKING TOWARDS.

What you want to achieve in life should be crazy fucking awesome so it only makes sense to have a wall dedicated to it!

Use your FUCKIT LIST, HEROIC QUOTES, SUPER SLOGANS, AND DECLUSTERFUCKING ROCKET to help you determine the imagery and whatever the heck else you want to showcase. Whip out that poster board (or two!) and go heckin' crazy on your wall.

Your Missions Should You Choose to Accept Them

YOU'VE GOT THIS. YOU'VE BLOODY WELL ACED YOUR COMBAT TRAINING AND HAVE ALL YOUR MISSIONS PLANNED OUT, READY TO SLAY. THERE WILL BE BLOOD, SWEAT AND TEARS, AND PROBABLY SOME ASSHATS TO CURB-STOMP. YOU HAVE EVERYTHING IT TAKES TO BE YOUR OWN SUPERHERO, AND TO FUCKING FIGHT FOR WHAT MATTERS TO YOU!

Do you understand that you're a badass superhero destined for greatness? Y N

Do you understand just how important your missions are? Y N

Do you understand that people are relying on you? Y N

Do you understand that these will be the toughest, most rewarding fights of your life? Y N

Do you accept your missions? Y N

THIS BOOK WILL SELF-DESTRUCT IN 5 SECONDS... just messing with you!

BREAKING NEWS
BREAK

We interrupt your (1)_________________________ for this breaking news...

It has been reported that over the last (2)_________________________ there have been several (3)_________________________ in the (4)_____________ vicinity.

The culprit is believed to be a (5)_______________ (6)_________________ wearing (7)_______________________and carrying a (8)___________.

This individual is extremely (9)___________. If you see them do not (10)________________ them, instead call (11)_________________________ immediately. Please stay safe and remain inside your (12)_______________.

For (13)________________ I'm (14)_________________________ and (15)_______________________.

LINE 1   a) sixth straight hour of Netflix binging b) afternoon slump c) declusterfucking

LINE 2   a) two lunar cycles b) fortnight c) New York minute

LINE 3   a) botched home haircuts b) toilet paper thefts c) coat hanger lobotomies

LINE 4   a) Winterfell b) Disneyland c) Florida

LINE 5   a) peg-legged b) weeping c) geriatric

LINE 6   a) hipster b) WWE wrestler c) soccer mom

LINE 7   a) a Paw Patrol backpack b) nothing but a cowboy hat c) a fluffy pink bunny onesie

LINE 8   a) baggie of magic beans b) dead cat c) Nerf gun

LINE 9   a) constipated b) sleep deprived c) sweaty

LINE 10   a) applaud b) blow kisses at c) do shots with

LINE 11   a) their mother b) the Fun Police c) loudly to your neighbour from the end of your driveway

LINE 12   a) pillow fort b) cowshed c) local IKEA

LINE 13   a) News in the Nude b) End Times Tonight c) WTF News

LINE 14   a) Norb Urdungy b) Ron Zombie c) The Queen of England

LINE 15   a) I'm about to climax b) I've got the munchies c) I have daddy issues

CH 5
LEAGUE OF EXTRAORDINARY
ASS-KICKING PEOPLE

MAKE YOUR L.E.A.P.

CONTRARY TO POPULAR BELIEF, YOU DON'T HAVE TO DO EVERYTHING ALONE.

THE MOST EPIC SUPERHEROES IN THE WORLD ROSE UP BECAUSE THEY HAD KICK-ASS TEAMS OF SIDEKICKS, GURUS, AND BUTLERS HELPING THEM BECOME THE BEST AT WHAT THEY DO.

YOU AIN'T GOT TIME FOR LAZY PROCRASTINAUTS ON YOUR TEAM! SURROUND YOURSELF WITH EXTRAORDINARY ASS-KICKING PEOPLE INSTEAD AND YOU'LL ALL GO FARTHER TOGETHER.

SO HOW DOES A SUPERHUMAN GO ABOUT RECRUITING SUCH A MOTLEY CREW? FIRST, THINK OF SOME SKILLS YOU'LL NEED TO ACQUIRE TO HELP YOU EXECUTE YOUR MISSION CRITICALS. NEED TO LEARN HOW TO PROPERLY LIFT WEIGHTS, BUILD A WEBSITE, OR IMPROVE YOUR PUBLIC SPEAKING CHOPS?

1. Reflect back on your MCs and list all the skills you can think of that you'll need to help you dominate.

2. What types of superhumans will you need on your team to help you accelerate your progress in these areas? Personal trainer, website designer, communications coach?

3. Spend some serious time researching who offers these skills and how you can involve them. Do you know anyone personally that can help?

MC NAME	SKILLS NEEDED	TYPE OF SUPERHUMAN	SPECIFIC SUPERHUMAN

Who's Got Your Back?

You become like the people you surround yourself with, so choose wisely when building your League of Extraordinary Ass-Kicking People (L.E.A.P.). Here's mine:

The Underdog

DESCRIPTION

Nerdy boxer with an eye for number-crunching and trash-talking math solutions in the ring. 2+2=4 motherfuckers!

SUPERPOWERS

Solves any problem you can throw at him – that includes changing your mommy's diapers. The harder the problem, the bigger The Underdog grows to overcome it. Watch out marshmallow man.

Donna Bionic

DESCRIPTION

One part endearing, cookie-baking granny, one part crime fighting, killing machine. She's fallen down the stairs so many times half her body has been replaced by robotic parts.

SUPERPOWERS

Barrel rolls down the stairs taking out any assholes in her way. Can pinch bad guys' cheeks so hard that they tear right off.

Disco Dave

DESCRIPTION

Smooth talker, shit-tons of confidence and makes chatting up strangers look like a breeze.

SUPERPOWERS

Can groove and move his body in all kinds of crazy directions. Dodges and dances around any bad guys' punches or bullets. Summons lightning with the power of his sexy hip thrusts.

Cheery Bomb

Super Caffeinated Coffee Man

Bitch Slayer

Smells like team spirit! This li'l cherry pie packs a sparkly punch of color in your day and puts a pep in your step with her sweet and sparkly optimism.

Bubbly and energetic, she'll instantly recharge your depleted spirit with one joyful little shimmy of her pom-poms. Amplifies the powers of every superhero around her and will make you unexplainably fucking cheerful as a ray of sunshine.

Do you like coffee? He likes coffee. He likes it so much he drinks five litres daily! Can't lose that coffee buzz or else he'll slip into a coma! Isn't coffee fucking GREAT?!

World's fastest coffee drinker! Never sleeps! Super productive! Can sense when those around him need a caffeine boost! What a guy!

She's spent centuries slaying vampires and zombies, and now she's after all them hateful snitches and bitches. Always has your back and takes no BS from anyone!

Inacts the will of justice with her mighty bitch stick upon those who spread hate, lies and bad vibes.

On the next page put together *your* L.E.A.P.

MY L.E.A.P.

THINK ABOUT THE HUMANS IN YOUR LIFE WHO INSPIRE YOU, HOLD YOU ACCOUNTABLE, AND ARE THERE FOR YOU IN TIMES OF BEWILDERMENT. WRITE DOWN ALL THOSE CLOSE TO YOU THAT YOU WANT TO KEEP ON YOUR TEAM, AND HAVE SOME FUN CREATING THEIR SUPERHERO NAME AND POWERS!

MY L.E.A.P.	SUPERHERO NAME	SUPERPOWERS	CHECKLIST SCORE

L.E.A.P. CHECKLIST

REALITY CHECK! EACH SUPERHERO YOU'VE CHOSEN TO BE ON YOUR TEAM SHOULD HAVE SIMILAR VALUES TO YOU. PONDER YOUR TEAMMATES, ANSWER THE BELOW QUESTIONS AND RATE THEM ON THE 5-POINT SCALE OF AWESOMENESS (USE PENCIL).

5 = FUCK YEAH! WITHOUT A DOUBT.
4 = YEAH, MOST OF THE TIME.
3 = SOMETIMES.
2 = RARELY.
1 = FUCK NO! THEY'D NEVER, EVER.

	1	2	3	4	5
1. They give me honest, constructive feedback.	1	2	3	4	5
2. They reject my bullshit excuses when I'm slacking.	1	2	3	4	5
3. They'd hold me accountable to achieve my MCs.	1	2	3	4	5
4. They'd be there for me during my toughest battles.	1	2	3	4	5
5. They keep my deepest, darkest secrets to themselves.	1	2	3	4	5
6. They always remain positive and hopeful about the future.	1	2	3	4	5
7. They'd say nothing but nice things about me to others.	1	2	3	4	5
8. They'd give me top-notch advice.	1	2	3	4	5
9. They'd grab a bullet out of mid-air for me.	1	2	3	4	5
10. They believe that I'm an extraordinary ass-kicking person.	1	2	3	4	5

43-50 = This level of awesomeness is as mind-blowing as a Category 5 hurricane. When shit hits the fan and all hell breaks loose, you know they've got your back. Keep close this glitterbomb of glory, treat them well, and tell them how much they mean to you cause you've snagged yourself a diamond in the rough!

33-42 = Your pal here is too legit to quit. Your relationship ain't perfect, but like a laser beam in the night, they still light up your world pretty bright. Think of how you could take this relationship to divine heights - they're worth your time and energy!

16-32 = Has potential to be on your team, but this relationship currently isn't as life-giving as it could be. You might make each other want to pull out your hair at times, but you usually find a way to hug it out. The reality is you might just be two very different personality types, and that's OK!

10-15 = A real dirtbag that has no beeswax being on your team! Be careful around this untrustworthy arse-nugget – they ooze selfishness and only look out for themselves. If you're thinking about trying to make this relationship work – stop! Ain't nobody got time for talking to a trash can.

CONNECTING WITH
SUPERHERO COMMUNITIES

WANT TO KNOW HOW TO CONNECT WITH OTHER SUPERHEROES JUST LIKE YOU?

1. Call them on a burner phone
2. Point a searchlight into the sky with their symbol on it
3. Telepathy
4. Hijack the radio or television
5. Become a photographer for the local newspaper and stalk them
6. Put yourself in mortal danger so they'll come to save you
7. Join the army's teleconference session with other superheroes

JUST KIDDING! Brainstorm some 'normal' ways you can get involved with other superheroes who are on a similar path to you. Get specific! *Some examples: Online communities, meet-ups you can join, relevant courses, coaching sessions, getting in touch with past coworkers, etc...*

Who are some real-life superheroes (experts, leaders, CEOs...) that you've dreamt of meeting?

Why is it important that you meet them? How could they help you?

TAKING DOWN THE
SOCIAL ANXIETY MONSTER

S.A.M. GOT YOU FEELING INSECURE, TIMID, AND A BIT PATHETIC? GENTLY SHOW THAT MONSTER HOW TO FUCK RIGHT OFF.

ATTACK 1: Pick up your phone and - *brace yourself!* - call at least one friend to have a real conversation with them. You know, the kind where you show genuine interest in each other's lives?

ATTACK 2: Participate in an online community related to something you're passionate about. Voice your opinion, say some stuff, and maybe even help someone out!

ATTACK 3: Ask for help and talk to a professional or someone in your L.E.A.P about this S.A.M. guy.

Do you struggle connecting with others at large gatherings? Sweat your pits off during small-talk one-on-one? Maybe you have Facebookaphobia? What are some areas where you need to take your social skills to the next level?

____

____

____

____

____

Who could you connect with that you maybe haven't spoken to in a while?

____

____

____

____

____

What are 2-3 actions you will take right now to lay an ass-kicking on the Social Anxiety Monster?

____

____

____

____

____

ADDING VALUE TO OTHERS

YOU HAVE SOME FUCKING AMAZING GIFTS TO OFFER THIS WORLD. WHEN YOU ADD VALUE (I.E. SELFLESSLY GIVE) TO THE LIVES OF OTHERS, YOU ALSO BENEFIT FROM LIVING A HAPPIER, MORE FULFILLING EXISTENCE CHOCK FULL OF LIFE-GIVING RELATIONSHIPS.

As you look back at your MCs there should be at least 1-2 that serve or enrich the lives of others. Summarize these ones below and think about the needs of the people they're serving.

Who is impacted by your MCs? Who is your target demographic to serve?

MC NAME	TARGET DEMOGRAPHIC	WHAT THEY NEED/CARE ABOUT

What value can you add to your L.E.A.P.? Think of small or big gestures that could make a difference in the lives of those closest to you.

____

____

____

____

____

SOMETIMES IN THE SKIRMISHES OF LIFE YOUR ASS GETS LIT ON FIRE FROM ALL THE BURNING PILES OF GARBAGE PITCHED YOUR WAY. IT AIN'T EASY TO PUT OUT EVERY FIRE ON YOUR OWN, SO HOPEFULLY YOU HAVE A SOLID **L.E.A.P.** TO HELP PUT OUT YOUR FLAMING MESSES.

Think of some of the burning assfires you've had in your life: Who was there to help you put them out?

____

____

____

____

____

____

____

____

____

____

Now go and thank those extraordinary beings for saving your ass.

NEVER FORGET THE IMPORTANCE OF APPRECIATING THOSE WHO'VE GOT YOUR BACKSIDE!

People I'd Like to Punch in the Face

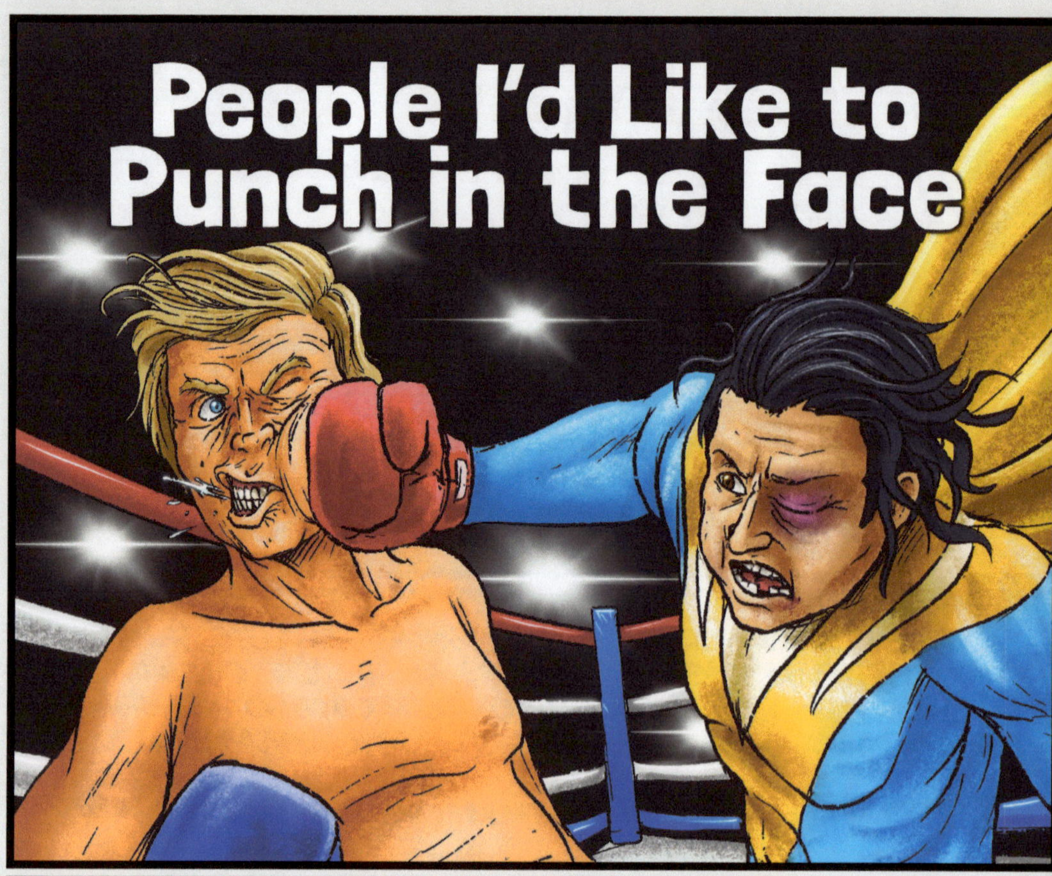

SOME PEOPLE ARE JUST EXASPERATING AF. DON'T YOU WISH YOU COULD JUST PUNCH THEM RIGHT IN THEIR STUPID FACE? NOTHING LIKE SOME GOOD OL' FASHIONED CATHARSIS!

Who are the people you'd like to punch in the face right now?

 Turning FOES Into FRIENDS

GENERALLY SPEAKING, IT'S BEST TO AVOID PEOPLE WHO HAVE A KNACK FOR MAKING YOU FEEL LIKE GARBAGE. MOST EVILDOERS YOU KNOW ARE LIKELY TOTAL ASSCLOWNS AND DEFINITELY DON'T DESERVE YOUR FRIENDSHIP, BUT... EVERY NOW AND THEN YOU'LL KNOW IN YOUR HEART THAT IT'S PROBABLY BEST TO TRY AND GET ALONG.

The goal of any superhero is not to completely obliterate their foes, but to help them become the best version of themselves again.

MAKE TIME TO HAVE A CONVERSATION WITH THEM AND DISCUSS THE ISSUES THAT STAND BETWEEN YOU. HAMMER THAT SHIT OUT, TELL THEM HOW YOU FEEL AND WHAT YOU ULTIMATELY WANT FROM YOUR RELATIONSHIP. IF IT'S WORTH FIGHTING FOR THEN PUT UP EVERY EFFORT TO MAKE IT WORK!

TO TURN FOES INTO FRIENDS, YOU'LL NEED TO BRACE YOURSELF FOR THE MOST CERTAIN CHALLENGES AHEAD.

Are there choppy relationships in your life that you wish would be more smooth sailing? Write 1–2 below:

____

What specific issues led to the relationship(s) getting to this point?

____

____

____

Where would you like the relationship(s) to ideally be?

____

____

____

What first small steps can you take to move it in that direction?

____

____

____

Finding Your Mary Jane or Bruce Wayne

THE GREATEST SUPERHERO SIDEKICK ONE COULD ASK FOR IS SOMEONE WHO WILL POSITIVI-WHIP YOU WHEN YOU'RE BEING NEGATIVE, DROP SOME TRUTH BOMBS WHEN YOU'RE OUT OF LINE, AND SMACK YOU IN THE FACE WITH A CHILL-OUT SURFBOARD WHEN YOU'VE LOST YOUR COOL.

WHETHER YOU HAVE THIS PERSON IN YOUR LIFE TODAY OR ARE STILL SEARCHING FOR YOUR MARY JANE OR BRUCE WAYNE, THEY COULD BE ONE OF THE MOST IMPORTANT PEOPLE IN YOUR L.E.A.P.

Create your **WOW** list for your ideal partner-in-crime below. Think about their traits, qualities, values, and appearance that would tickle you pink (and anything else you can think of).

If you already have a partner, still create a **WOW** list and under the 'Others' Needs' column, think about what your partner needs. Even the best relationship gurus still gotta work at being the ultimate sex magnets for their partners, and you should too!

W   O   W

WHAT I NEED	OTHERS' NEEDS	WHAT I CAN GIVE

Never underestimate the power of WOW!

Kicking Ass and Taking Names

"There are no perfect journeys in life. There are dead ends, we take the wrong exits, and we lose all the fucking air in our tires. The good news is, it doesn't matter what kind of fresh hell the journey looks like. What matters is that you choose a road, enjoy the ride, and don't get stuck in one place."
— Bravebud

BALLS TO THE WALL

PURSUING ANYTHING WORTHWHILE IN LIFE DEMANDS THAT YOU GO **BALLS TO THE WALL!** IF YOU'RE NOT SEEING MUCH PROGRESS IN THE BEGINNING, DON'T GET DOWN ON YOURSELF; IT'LL COME WITH TIME AND MAXIMUM EFFORT.

SO DON'T FUCKING GIVE UP NOW!

Balls to the Wall
When an airplane pilot needs full power, they move the throttle (which has a **ball**-shaped top) forward towards the front **wall** of the cockpit (aka a firewall); to exude maximum effort; to go all out.

Out of 10, how would you rank your current effort levels on your MCs? (Re-evaluate yourself and complete this list every 1–3 months)

MC NAME	SCORE (Out of 10)	WHAT I NEED TO DO TO GET TO 10

HEY,
SUPERHUMAN! THIS IS YOUR TIME TO REFLECT ON ALL THAT YOU'VE BEEN WORKING TOWARDS.

YOU'VE SEEN IT THROUGHOUT THIS JOURNAL: GET SHIT DONE BY FIRST GETTING YOUR MIND, BODY, AND ENVIRONMENT RIGHT. ONCE YOU'VE GOT THESE DOWN, THERE'S NO STOPPING YOU FROM GETTING THE MOST OUT OF YOUR SUPERPOWERS!

ARE YOU MAKING SOME IMPORTANT SHIT HAPPEN?

THE MOST EFFECTIVE WAY TO EXECUTE ON WHAT YOU WANT TO ACCOMPLISH IS TO HAVE AN ORGANIZED PLAN LAID OUT AHEAD OF YOU. USE THIS WORKSHEET ON THE RIGHT TO ORGANIZE A MEAL PLAN FOR YOUR WEEK, GET YOUR PHYSICAL FITNESS ROUTINES IN CHECK, AND TO CREATE A DAILY MENTAL WELLNESS ROUTINE THAT'S FULL OF GOOD VIBES.

WEEKLY FEELIN' DAMN GOOD PLAN

	BREAKFAST	LUNCH	SNACKS	DINNER
S				
M				
T				
W				
T				
F				
S				

Daily SWEAT MY ASS OFF Plan

	S	M	T	W	T	F	S
Wk 1							
Wk 2							
Wk 3							
Wk 4							

Daily GOOD VIBES

S	
M	
T	
W	
T	
F	
S	

Let's GET SHIT DONE!

THE BEST WAY TO OWN YOUR DAY LIKE A BOSS IS TO GET YOURSELF HOOKED ON HAVING DOPE-ASS DAILY ROUTINES TO HELP YOU GET SHIT DONE! HAVING AN ORGANIZED SCHEDULE FILLED WITH ROUTINES THAT POSITIVELY PROPEL YOU CLOSER TO FEELING GOOD AND ACHIEVING YOUR MISSION CRITICALS IS EXACTLY WHAT WE'RE TALKING ABOUT HERE.

1. Start by taking your Heroic Habits in Chapter 4 and organize them into one of three time blocks in your day: Grab Your Morning by the Balls, Mid-Day Slay, and Nighttime Primetime.

2. Add in any other actions from your 'Feelin' Damn Good Plan' or any of the other exercises in this book that will positively impact your day.

3. Take your list from below and organize them into time slots on the right. Color the bubbles in on the right if it's a routine that you'll complete on that day. Leave them blank if that's a day off from that routine.

4. When you complete your routine, check it off in the bubble for that day.

Grab Your Morning by the Balls	Mid-Day Slay	Nighttime Primetime

Routines for GETTING SHIT DONE

Grab Your Morning By the Balls Routines

TIME	TASK		S M T W T F S
			◯◯◯◯◯◯◯
			◯◯◯◯◯◯◯
			◯◯◯◯◯◯◯
			◯◯◯◯◯◯◯
			◯◯◯◯◯◯◯
			◯◯◯◯◯◯◯
			◯◯◯◯◯◯◯
			◯◯◯◯◯◯◯

Mid-Day Slay Routines

		S M T W T F S
		◯◯◯◯◯◯◯
		◯◯◯◯◯◯◯
		◯◯◯◯◯◯◯
		◯◯◯◯◯◯◯
		◯◯◯◯◯◯◯
		◯◯◯◯◯◯◯

Nighttime Primetime Routines

		S M T W T F S
		◯◯◯◯◯◯◯
		◯◯◯◯◯◯◯
		◯◯◯◯◯◯◯
		◯◯◯◯◯◯◯
		◯◯◯◯◯◯◯
		◯◯◯◯◯◯◯
		◯◯◯◯◯◯◯

CRYO FREEZE

LIFE MOVES BY TOO DAMN QUICKLY! ONE MOMENT YOU'RE A KID BLOWING BUBBLES IN YOUR MILK AND THE NEXT YOU'RE WEARING ADULT DIAPERS. WE OFTEN GET SO FOCUSED ON OUR END GOALS THAT WE FORGET TO NOTICE ALL THE MAGICAL THINGS HAPPENING DURING THE PROCESS OF REACHING THEM.

Revisit some of the accomplishments you've made so far on your MCs. How would you like to celebrate or freeze some of these majestic moments in time? Think about celebrations, fancy parties, plaques, framed pictures, or anything else you can do to make your accomplishments truly memorable.

MC NAME	CRYO FREEZE CELEBRATIONS

Life is Like a Ticking Time Bomb

HAVE YOU HEARD YOURSELF OR SOMEONE ELSE SAY 'SOMEDAY' I'LL DO THAT TRIP OR 'SOMEDAY' I'LL FULFILL THAT DREAM? **SCREW SOMEDAY!**

The reality is life is like a ticking time bomb: you never know when the next zombie apocalypse or worldwide pandemic will sidetrack your life.

Think about the next year ahead of you: What accomplishments and MCs will you celebrate one year from today? (Rank them in order of importance)

____

____

____

____

____

____

____

____

Unmasking Your Secret Identity

MANY SUPERHUMANS LIVE A LIFE THAT ISN'T REFLECTIVE OF WHOM THEY TRULY ARE. THEY DO THE DAILY GRIND OF A SOUL-CRUSHING 9 TO 5, FULFILLING SOMEONE ELSE'S AGENDA. EAT, SLEEP, WORK, REPEAT.

WORK SHOULD BE ENGAGING, INSPIRING, AND BALL/TITTY TINGLING. IT SHOULD MAKE YOU SAY:

IF YOU'RE NOT FEELING THIS SENSATION THEN IT'S HIGH TIME YOU THINK ABOUT HOW TO MAKE THIS YOUR REALITY.

DECIDING WHEN TO TELL YOUR BOSS, COWORKERS, FRIENDS AND FAMILY THAT YOU'RE DESTINED FOR SOMETHING GREATER IS A DIFFICULT DECISION FOR ANY SUPERHERO.

SO WHEN'S THE RIGHT TIME FOR YOU TO QUIT YOUR DAY JOB AND BECOME A FULL-TIME SUPERHERO PURSUING WHAT'S MEANINGFUL TO YOU?

On the next two pages are 27 questions to help give you an idea of how close you are to being able to kick your 9 to 5 and focus on your big badass dreams.

STRESS AND WELL-BEING

1. Do you have time to work out 3-5 times per week? (Y) (N)
2. Do you have time to cook healthy meals 3-5 times per week? (Y) (N)
3. Do you bring stress from your day job home with you? (Y) (N)
4. Do you find yourself constantly complaining about your job to friends and family? (Y) (N)
5. Are you satisfied with your daily commute to work? (Y) (N)

WORKPLACE MISSION AND VALUES

6. Are you passionate about how your company serves the world? (Y) (N)
7. Do you know your company values and do they align with your personal values? (Y) (N)
8. Are you excited about the direction of your company? (Y) (N)
9. Do you see yourself in this workplace 5 years from now? (Y) (N)

ROLE FIT

10. Are you able to use your strengths and talents (your superpowers) at work on a regular basis? (Y) (N)
11. Do you wake up excited to go to work? (Y) (N)
12. Do you find yourself losing track of time at work because your job is so much fun? (Y) (N)
13. Is there another role within your company that would align with the type of work you'd love to do? (Y) (N)
14. Are you learning and growing within your current role? (Y) (N)
15. Are you given the opportunity to learn about topics that you're interested in at work? (Y) (N)

RELATIONSHIP WITH YOUR BOSS AND COWORKERS

16. Would you put your boss in your L.E.A.P.? (Y) (N)
17. Do you feel appreciated for your work? (Y) (N)
18. Do you enjoy working with your team of coworkers? (Y) (N)
19. Do you have any coworkers that belong in your L.E.A.P.? (Y) (N)

YOUR PERSONAL PURPOSE AND JOB ALIGNMENT

20. Can you clearly tell someone what your personal purpose is and what type of work you'd love to do? (Y) (N)
21. Do you have personal goals (Mission Criticals) to help you find and do work that you'd love? (Y) (N)
22. Can you start pursuing your purpose and still work at your current job? (Y) (N)

23. Do you have encouraging superhumans in your life that would support you if you decide to quit your job and pursue your purpose? (Y) (N)

24. Do you have friends, family or connections that will hold you accountable and push you to be better? (Y) (N)

FINANCES

25. Can you afford to quit your job and go at least 6 months without a pay check? (Y) (N)

26. Do you have a clear 'World Domination Plan' for how you will make money from the work you love doing within the next 6 months? (Y) (N)

27. Are you making enough money from your Mission Criticals or any other side hustles to cover your basic expenses (food, fuel, mortgage, car payments)? (Y) (N)

SCORING

Section	Score a Point for Answering YES to these questions	Score a Point for Answering NO to these questions	Points
Stress and Well-Being	3, 4	1, 2, 5	
Workplace Mission and Values		6, 7, 8, 9	
Role Fit		10, 11, 12, 13, 14, 15	
Relationship with Your Boss and Coworkers		16, 17, 18, 19	
Your Personal Purpose and Job Alignment	20, 21, 22		
Your L.E.A.P.	23, 24		
Finances	25, 26, 27		
		TOTAL POINTS	

25–27 POINTS: *Stick it to the Man!* - Looks like you're in a great spot to leave your day job and start pursuing your superhero side hustle! Ultimately, you're not going to find fulfillment continuing to work for a company that doesn't support your talents, purpose or well-being. Your finances are in tip-top shape and you're already making a few bucks doing what you love. You've got a supportive group of people that will have your back if you decide to quit. It's your call but all signs seem to point towards you sticking it to the man!

20–24 POINTS: *Shit's About to Get Real* - You're just about ready to quit your gig. Have a look at the sections where you scored low and figure out if there's any way to turn that shit around. If you've made every effort to address your concerns about your role with your boss, or you've switched up your role and responsibilities and things are still going south, it may be time for you to move on.

11–19 POINTS: *Some Shit to Sort Out* - It would be quite the bold move to quit at this juncture. You just might be in the right company/role to pursue your superhero goals, but perhaps a few minor things need to be tweaked in order for you to be in your sweet spot. Put in the effort to figure that shit out before you decide to pull the plug!

0–10 POINTS: *That's Some Good Shit* - You've got it pretty damn good where you are! You're part of a company or in a role where you get to use your brilliant talents for the good of humankind. It's clear that happiness and fulfillment surrounds you in all that you do.

First US Donkey
Elected President
MONTH DAY YEAR HOUR
04 22 2017 1305
DESTINATION TIME

The Time Machine

Pretend you have a time machine that could take you on a most excellent adventure to relive yesterday.

What made the day most excellent?

What habits worked well?

What habits do you need to adjust to improve for future days?

FUCK the F-WORD

WHEN WE HEAR THE WORD 'FAILURE' OUR BODIES AUTOMATICALLY RESPOND WITH ALL KINDS OF NEGATIVE FEELINGS IN OUR GUT. SAY OUT LOUD RIGHT NOW "I'M A FAILURE" AND WOULDN'T YOU KNOW - THAT PROBABLY MADE YOU FEEL LIKE SHIT!

AS A SOCIETY OF EXTRAORDINARY ASS-KICKING PEOPLE, WE NEED TO START LOOKING AT FAILURE IN A POSITIVE WAY. FAILURE TRULY IS THE BEST WAY FOR YOU TO LEARN AND GROW. AT SOME POINT IN EVERY SUPERHERO'S STORY, THEY'VE FAILED MISERABLY ONLY TO RISE UP AND DEFEAT THEIR OPPRESSOR. LOOK AT ANY PERCEIVED 'FAILURE' IN YOUR LIFE AS AN OPPORTUNITY TO DO THE SAME!

MAKE FAILURE FUN AGAIN! Below are some dope-ass phrases to replace the **F-word** that you can use in your everyday jargon. Go ahead and add a few of your favorites:

FUBAR
fucked up beyond all recognition

shitshow

screwed the pooch

HOSE JOB

FIASCO

LIMP DICKED IT

HOT MESS **shit hit the fan**

SNAFU - situation normal all fucked up

Write down some scenarios where you wet the bed, screwed the pooch, or limp dicked your way through something, and what you learned from those situations.

____

____

____

____

____

WE ALL GET KNOCKED DOWN FROM TIME TO TIME, BUT DAMN, DOES IT EVER HURT LIKE A **BITCH!** IT'S YOUR CHOICE, HOWEVER, WHETHER TO STAY ON THE GROUND OR PEEL YOURSELF OFF THE PAVEMENT TO SLAY ANOTHER DAY!

What specifically keeps knocking you down or getting in your way from owning your MCs?

____

____

____

____

____

Summarize some strategies to dodge these blows in the future.

____

____

____

____

____

Awards of Ass-Kicking Awesomeness

You get an award, you get an award... *you all get an award!*

THERE ARE TONS OF PEOPLE IN YOUR LIFE WHO DESERVE TO BE RECOGNIZED FOR BEING TOTALLY FUCKING AWESOME. NOMINATE THOSE SUPERHUMANS WHO DESERVE TO WIN THESE AWARDS - YOURSELF INCLUDED!

TAKE NO SHIT AWARD: For the person who doesn't take shit from nobody!

KEEPING IT REAL AWARD: For the person who gives it to you straight, and is always trusted to be completely honest with you.

SEXY IN SPANDEX AWARD: Honors that special someone whose hiney looks best when shiny.

THE UNDERDOG AWARD: For the person who gets knocked down, but always gets back up!

BEST SIDEKICK AWARD: For the person who's always got your back, even when it's sweaty.

PEE-PEE IN MY PANTS AWARD: For the person who always makes you laugh hard enough to pee a little.

BALLS TO THE WALL AWARD: For the person who hustles and bustles until the job gets DONE.

WORLD DOMINATION AWARD: For a superhero who is changing the world and making a massive difference in the lives of others!

Now go and let these folks know just how *ASS-KICKINGLY AWESOME* they truly are!

What is the meaning of life?

The answer is pretty simple: **YOU** are the meaning of life.

Ultimately, _you_ decide the meaning you want to give things in life, so _you_ decide the meaning of your journey. That meaning is uniquely yours, and won't be the same as anyone else's. The next question to ask is:

What is life?

Life is what you make of it. You decide how to live each moment and have the opportunity to define what those moments mean.

Maybe you haven't made all the best choices in life, but that doesn't matter. You can't change your origin story, but you _can_ choose to learn from it and let it make you stronger.

You are the one that holds the pen to the pages of your story. _You_ get to write in the bold and unexpected plot twists. Maybe completing this journal was one of them.

Maybe you love cooking for others or maybe you love Youtubing about ASMR or maybe you enjoy working in a sewage refinery.

Find your P.O.O.
(Plains of Otherworldliness)

Hunt down and discover what it is that makes you happy. It's up to you to find your meaning in life and fight for it. Life is a journey and not a destination.

"Life Doesn't Give Us Purpose, We Give Life Purpose."
-The Flash

Visit Bravebud.com to access exclusive content and join our League of Extraordinary Ass-Kicking People!

Plains of Otherworldliness

Lexicon of Badassery

1. **Plains of Otherworldliness:** A magical and mystical place, often mentioned in folklore, where you're finally doing the thing that you're meant to do with your life. Produces tingly sensations of glorious euphoria, not unlike that of blissfully sauntering through a glistening, dewy meadow as your fingertips deftly brush the tips of the pussy willows, all the while leaping and bounding your way towards that celestial pot of gold at the end of a rainbow.

2. **Big Explosive Brain Dump:** The dumping out of all thoughts, ideas, and discombobulated shit in your brain unto a paper vessel.

3. **Fight Club:** Dude... what part of "dO nOt TaLk AbOuT fIgHt ClUb" do you not understand?!?

4. **Energy Zombies:** People who drain the life out of a room with their need to feed off of negativity.

5. **Shit-For-Brains:** When every emotion, thought and feeling that your brain conjures up is just complete shit.

6. **Panic Room:** A special place where you can shield yourself from the plethora of worldly distractions and just get shit done.

7. **Declusterfucking:** The magical art of pulling all the jumbled up thoughts out of your brain, dumping them out on paper and organizing them into happy little clusters.

8. **Mission Criticals:** Your absolutes, your musts, and your unwavering will-do's.

9. **Declusterfucking Rocket of Happiness:** Your group of Mission Criticals that will launch you towards a life of otherworldliness full of purpose, fulfillment and happiness.

10. **Milestoning:** The act of smashing your Mission Criticals into itty-bitty steps that are measurable, date specific and easier to attain.

11. **Happy Endings:** The goal of all superhero stories; the end result of achieving your Mission Criticals.

12. **Heroic Habits:** The art of breaking down your goal into small daily Habits, Fire-Starters, and Rewardgasms.

13. **Fire-Starters:** The visual cues/triggers you set in place that automatically remind you to complete a habit.

14. **Rewardgasms:** The rewards that would actually turn you on to complete your habits every day.

15. **Balls to the Wall:** Originating in aviation, when a pilot needs full power, they move the throttle (which has a ball-shaped top) forward towards the front wall of the cockpit (aka a firewall); to exude maximum effort; to go all out.

16. **SUPERJOURNAL:** Your sacred text to guide you along a kick-ass journey of getting shit done, making the world a better a place and becoming the badass superhero you truly are.